Notes
from the
Firehouse

A Collection of Stories
About Life as a Firefighter

D. E. McCourt

Notes from the Firehouse: A Collection of Stories about Life as a Firefighter © 2011 by D. E. McCourt

Published by McCourt Movers
4 Suntaug St., Lynnfield, MA 01940

Web site: www.notesfromthefirehouse.com

Manufactured in the United States of America

ISBN-10: 1452872392
EAN-13: 9781452872391
Library of Congress Control Number: 2010908816

10 9 8 7 6 5 4 3 2 1

Editorial Consultant: Edward D. McCourt, Professor, Jacksonville University
Front Cover Design by Kathryn Jones, KJ Imaging Associates
Cover Photo courtesy of Chickie McCarthy, Melrose Fire
Interior & Back Cover Design by Jill Ronsley, Sun Editing & Book Design
Special thanks to my sister, Pat Savani, for all her encouragement and support

In memory of

Edward A. McCourt

CONTENTS

INTRODUCTION

THERE ARE COUNTLESS ACTS of humanity performed by firefighters on a daily basis. Some are small, almost trivial things that only have meaning to the people involved, others are life-altering experiences that never gain the public's attention unless there is enough drama to sell newspapers.

The Hollywood stereotypes of the job are misleading to say the least. I have never seen a Dalmatian in a fire truck, never rescued a cat from a tree. I've never carried a person out of a burning building or seen a burning vehicle explode like an atom bomb. Those things may occur, but that's not the job. For the average firefighters it's about the hours spent around the station trying not to get on each others' nerves and the random nonsense that always seems to infiltrate that void. It's about the countless false alarms and nuisance calls that we respond to with an irritating regularity. These things are a very real part of the job, and yet that's not why the city pays us. No, we're there for the hair-raising moments, the gut-wrenching scenes and the dirty work.

The fire department is like a security blanket that helps citizens sleep at night; they know if the unthinkable ever happens there is someone to call for help. If and when that call is made, we respond to it like no other government agency. No red tape, nothing to be taken under advisement, just a simple call brings immediate action. Now that's tax dollars at work. Need the help of a dozen people? We'll be there in a few minutes. What, you need more help than that? Give us another five minutes and watch and listen. It's a service you hope you'll never need, but most people are amazed at the response they get when they do.

The stories I recount are no different than those of a thousand other firefighters. The human condition is basically the same everywhere. The outrageous humor found in the firehouses where I worked is probably very similar to those in Albuquerque, Miami or anywhere else. The calls we answer aren't much different either. Some respond to more fires, while others respond to more medical-aids or motor vehicle accidents.

To a firefighter it all amounts to the same thing: responding to a call for help. We stand by and watch as these countless calls to action slip into the past without song or ceremony. Instead, the only record that remains is a simple entry in a large generic journal. A few terse lines that only record times, addresses and descriptions—such as house fire or medical-aid. Lines that will never document the humanity displayed by firefighters who always deflect any attention by saying, "We were just doing our job." As a participant you feel a responsibility to remember those events, those individuals and what transpired before it all disappears into the past forever.

CLOSER THAN I KNEW

IN ONE WAY OR another, every profession is influenced by the economy. From Wall Street brokers to city workers, nobody gets a free pass. A bad economy is like a ripple in a pond that eventually rocks every boat. The fire department is somewhat different in its response to fiscal problems. We don't create money or operate on a profit margin. Yet soaring interest rates and high unemployment can affect our profession in some rather unusual ways. For instance, bad economic times can mean more runs for the fire department. Perhaps in the form of medical aids due to the financial stress, or problems with space heaters where money is being saved on heat or a host of other things that, at first glance, might not seem related to a downturn in the business cycle. The worse side effect of a bad economy for firefighters is an increase in the number of arson incidents. The most dreaded of these are the botched attempts of arsonists who really don't understand the unpredictable nature of fire.

Arson that is caused by a failing economy is carried out with the intent of the fire destroying the house, vehicle or any other property, along with all the evidence of the crime, before firefighters can arrive, but that is not always the case. It's just not that simple. For one thing, the nature of combustibles is not as cut and dried as one may think. Another is the timing of the deed, which can be hard to control, yet absolutely critical to an arsonist. The arsonist needs to start a fire, usually with an accelerant, but must vacate the area before anybody is aware of the blaze. Anyone who has ever attempted lighting even a simple barbecue with a flammable fluid knows that sometimes a match can produce much more fire than expected, then just as quickly die out. Multiply that unpredictability by a hundred and you can begin to understand the dilemma of the novice arsonist. The resulting flames and smoke have a way of grabbing everyone's attention, which is the last thing someone committing a felony needs before they've had a chance to flee the area. So the tricky part of the equation is this: the fire must be intense enough to completely destroy the unwanted property before the local heroes can arrive and put it out. Here is where a novice arsonist can make a critical mistake. Some of them vastly underestimate the response time of the nearest fire department and that's a problem for the firefighters, as well as the arsonist.

The recession had been triggered by higher interest rates. Raising interest rates was suppose to subdue inflation, but it created chaos in the economy as well. Housing starts were almost down to zero. Existing houses were not moving at all unless they were sold for far less than the owner expected. Contractors and real estate firms were all barely surviving. Many would fold under the pressure before things turned around. It was from the financially trapped and the impatient sellers that arson would soon appear.

A call for a house fire was received by the dispatcher in the early morning hours. A time when a fire may not be detected until it has had a chance to become fully involved in the structure and the possibility of someone accidentally witnessing the crime is very low. The box assignment called for three engines, a ladder and a rescue. In this town, the response time of the first engine would be rapid.

Everyone, in fact, would be off at the scene within minutes of receiving the alarm. The house turned out to be a vacant single family home with heavy smoke showing on all sides.

Firefighters felt relieved that the building was unoccupied, which is always a blessing. Yet, from a firefighter's point of view, even to save the actual house is something worth risking bodily harm. We don't check the fire insurance policy before we attempt to save a house from devastation. This could be somebody's nest egg or the equity it holds could be a college education for someone's children. There is no way of knowing at 1.00 a.m. in the morning if the house is under-insured, or if perhaps the policy is lapsed and there isn't any insurance at all. But every blue-collared one of us knows what it would be like to lose the largest asset that most of us will ever own. So firefighters take a risk to save a building that, in their minds, personifies someone's health and welfare, just as it would their own.

Firefighter Eddie Mac and the rescue company entered the house with this particular frame of mind. A vacant house allowed the rescue company to work the fire with everyone else. No search and rescue on this one, just straight-up firefighting. The house was completely charged with smoke. Visibility was almost zero. Outside, the ladder company vented the roof, while inside, firefighters were cleaning out windows trying to relieve the smoky conditions.

Fire was found in various parts of the building and on both the first and second floors. Mac and the rescue company knocked down the fire on the second floor, while on the first the situation was quickly being brought under control. It seemed more than a little odd that the second-floor fire was located nowhere near the first-floor fire. As windows were opened or broken and the smoke escaped through the vented roof, the atmosphere inside the house began to slowly clear. Mac worked at pulling down a ceiling around a light fixture where something incendiary might have hung. Others on the first floor were finding similar situations as it became apparent that the fire was set.

Mac continued to open up a wall, working to make sure there were no hot spots left inside to smolder. What he didn't know was that below him on the first floor was a bathroom tub filled with gasoline, which somehow had yet to be ignited. Since everyone was wearing breathing apparatus, no one had even smelled the fumes. Suddenly, the vapors ignited, triggering a massive explosion. Mac, still working at pulling plaster upstairs, was dazed by the shock wave of the blast. The gasoline, still in liquid form, was blown up through the opening he had just made in a wall and the liquid completely drenched him. Burning embers still present in the room immediately set him ablaze. Mac regained his senses after the blast and in disbelief he saw himself totally engulfed in flames. His mind began to race. His first thought was, "I'm dead!" Suddenly, he remembered the door to the room lead directly to the staircase from the first floor. In desperation, he turned and ran through the door and dove down the flight of stairs, as if he were diving into a pond. A firefighter ascending the stairs was knocked down by this human torch flying through the air. The firefighter quickly recovered and attempted to put out the flames enveloping Mac, and with his own body pinned Mac to the floor. Other firefighters joined him and completely smothered the remaining fire.

The firefighters instantly removed Mac from the building and then gathered around him, as he was laid upon the ground in front of the house. He rose to his feet, despite protests, and started to take off his gear, which was hot and still smoking. The men removed it for him, while trying not to let him move about too much. Once he was freed from his gear, they attempted to set him on a rescue cot. But he would have none of it, insisting no fuss was necessary. Yet one look at him told all of them that he was in shock and didn't realize the extent of his own injuries. The ranking officer insisted that he go to the hospital and at least get checked out, in a tone that implied that it was an order, rather than a request. Reluctantly, Mac sat on the cot and he was loaded into the rescue truck for a quick ride to a nearby hospital. He felt a little embarrassed by all the attention.

This embarrassment soon faded as the initial shock wore off and indescribable pain took over instead. His ears and neck, as well as the tops of his thighs, started burning, as if the fire was still there. Each moment, the pain seemed to get worse. "Damn that hurts," he said through clenched teeth, as the pain reached a new level. One of the firefighters on the rescue poured sterile water over the burned areas, trying to ease the pain. His pants were cut away to expose his burned thighs. The sterile water offered little relief but it felt better than nothing at all. His fellow firefighters wished they had gallons of it, even if it only helped a little bit. It was painful for them to watch one of their own suffer like this.

Evidently, the ear flaps of his helmet were not on tight, so his ears and neck were burned. His legs were burned when the gas splashed between his coat and the tops of his boots, an area that was hard to protect with the old-style gear. The key piece of protection he was wearing worked perfectly, without his breathing apparatus he would have been dead in an instant. His lungs would have been destroyed by the time they put out the flames. Ironically, the pain he felt was a good sign. The nerve endings were still functioning so the burns were bad, but second degree, not third.

The quick actions of his fellow firefighters had saved him from the devastation of third-degree burns. At that moment, this information was of no consolation to a man suffering from the agony of burnt flesh. But later on it would be greatly appreciated and remembered. A few hours later, Mac's wife, Barbara, received an early morning visitor. It was a deputy from the fire department, who also happened to be an old friend of the family.

As he entered the house, Barbara noticed Eddie wasn't with him and she thought to herself, "It's a little early for a social call." Quickly, she looked into his face and from his serious expression she knew something bad had happened. Seeing the flash of fear in her eyes the deputy assured her that Mac was okay. He told her, "Ed has been hurt at a fire, but is in no danger now and is resting at the hospital. Don't worry, Barbara, he's okay." She felt her heart begin to beat a little more normally as he explained the extent and nature of the injuries.

The deputy offered to drive her to the hospital, but she had children to get ready for school. She would rather visit him alone the first time. Before leaving, he told her that he'd drop back later with Mac's car, which was still parked at the station, so she could visit him while the kids were in school. For the time being, she kept the knowledge of the injuries to herself, until she could visit with Ed and see for herself how he was doing.

After school, the kids were told about the situation and taken to the hospital to see their father. I am the second eldest of the four children and Eddie Mac is my father. Mac is just a firehouse nickname for McCourt. I remember at the time it wasn't a very dramatic visit at all. My father made light of the whole event and his wounds were mostly hidden by gauze dressings. Both of my parents seemed cheerful, but maybe it was just relief. Yet I still detected an underlying seriousness in their eyes. I'm sure if I had seen my father ablaze and writhing in pain I would have been absolutely horrified. But this wasn't the case and he gave no indication that anything that drastic had happened.

It turned out that a real estate company owned the house that they had tried to save that night. The market had turned sour and I guess somebody didn't want to take the loss. A firefighter with a wife and four children almost took a much bigger loss because of someone's greed. Back then, an arson investigation wasn't nearly as in depth as it is today. Most of the science used to catch an arsonist just didn't exist. No charges were ever filed.

Looking back, I might wonder why my father prodded me into taking the civil service examination to become a firefighter, but after all these years on the job I already know the answer. First of all, the job can be fun. At times, the firehouse can be more like a fraternity house than a workplace. Sometimes, you go to work expecting to be entertained, rather than worked, and then you're downright disappointed if you're not. Just driving down the street in the engine can bring a smile to your face, when all the children run and wave as you pass, and the elderly folks all greet you with a nod and smile. Over the years, they've needed help at one time or another, and the fire department has been there for them. I could never add up all the "God bless you guys," or the "Thank God for the fire department," blessings that citizens have bestowed on us over the years. I've often said if the voting age was limited to people over sixty-five and under twenty, we would be the highest-paid employees in the city. None of these things will ever show up in your pay check, but I truly believe these are some of the cherished benefits of the job.

My father is retired from the job now, his only permanent disability is a hearing loss from the wailing sirens and clanging bells, but almost every firefighter will end up with that problem. My brother, Dave, and I are both firefighters but in different towns. At family get-togethers, there is never a lack of conversation. We just tap into an endless supply of firefighting stories and usually end up trying to top one another's tale. Firefighting can be a very dangerous profession, but taking those chances while trying to help people somehow seems to justify the risks. The job has a way of making the perils worthwhile. My father always felt that way and after working the job for years, I have to agree.

Postscript: My father, Edward A. McCourt, died of an aneurysm on March 17, 1999, at the age of seventy-one. It was a shock to our family and St. Patrick's Day will never be the same for any of us. We were supposed to be eating a traditional boiled dinner at my brother Dave's house. Instead, we stood by my father's side as the life support systems keeping him alive were terminated, and watched the light leave the lamp of the man that we loved so much. A few minutes earlier, I had asked if I could spend some time alone in the room with him before he died. I held his hand while saying some prayers, then kissed him on the cheek and thanked him for everything he had done for me. I probably hadn't kissed him since I was six years old. So again, let me say, "Thank you, Dad," your extraordinary example of decency and compassion still guides me in a quiet compelling voice.

Batman

WHEN YOU BECOME A firefighter in the suburbs, the job is a little different than in a large metropolitan area. In a major city, the anarchy of the day may control what firefighters will or will not do on any given shift. Yet no one should think that every firehouse in a big city is the same. Yes, they have stations that do an incredible amount of runs, but they also have a few quiet stations, too. Usually, you'll find them tucked away in one of the wealthier parts of the city, where the property values are high and the crime is low. Most of the quiet stations have been given appropriate nicknames, such as *the farm* or *the country club*, because they do far fewer runs than most of their compadres. So don't think because someone works in Chicago or Boston they have to eat their lunch on the back of an engine because they're so busy. Instead, ask them which station they work at, because some of their stations are just like the *burbs*.

Yet, the busiest stations always seem to set the tone for any department, so the slower pace found in suburbia has a different atmosphere. This extra time is used judiciously in practicing the arts of fooling around, complaining and avoiding any job that the higher-ups try to trap us into doing, along with a wagon-full of other nonsense. The reality of it is this: our fires are just as hot and our motor vehicle accidents are just as gory, it's just that we have fewer of them. This extra time lends a weird dimension to our job, perhaps one that big city firefighters may never encounter. Whether this is a good or bad thing is a matter of conjecture. All I know is that in "Suburban Fire USA" we can fill this extra time with some pretty ridiculous situations.

The officers at the firehouse, like all firefighters, become bored at times. Sometimes, there's nothing on television, all the snacks brought to work have been eaten and, worst of all, the firefighters are creating a tumultuous roar in the day room. Some of the officers know they are born leaders if only given half a chance, but there are times when things are just plain quiet. So when a citizen calls and asks for help retrieving a renegade parrot from a large oak tree, it seems like just the thing to do. It may not be what the brass was hoping for, but at least they can assemble the troops and exercise some leadership.

This was the case when Engine 1 arrived on the scene of the "bird that flew the coop call." The situation was pretty straightforward: one colorful bird in one very large tree. The bird was much too high for the ground ladders the engine is equipped with, so naturally the ladder truck company was called to the scene for assistance. I was on the rescue company that day and I still don't know why the captain sent for us. Perhaps the bird was in distress or maybe he was just afraid to leave us alone for any length of time at the station.

Eight firefighters stood around the base of the tree and watched as the ladder company slowly maneuvered the aerial ladder to within a few feet of the rather subdued parrot. Onlookers had gathered below to witness the unusual event. A civilian standing next to me raised his eyebrows and asked, "What do ya think?" "My money is on the bird," I replied without cracking a smile. It's not every day you get to see a parrot rescue.

Up went one of the senior men of our department, and with great stealth he climbed until the parrot was within an arm's length. Then with a slow deliberate movement he extended his hands until they were just a few inches from the colorful prey. The parrot waited until the last possible second and with great nonchalance flew to another branch a few feet away, but just out of reach. So once again the process was repeated and this time with even more care. The ladder was repositioned and our man, with the utmost stealth, came to within inches of the feathered escapee, but as before, the bird calmly hopped to a branch slightly out of reach. Now, I can't be sure, but I believe the parrot knew what he was doing—or at least it looked that way. By flying just a few feet away, the ham was leading us on and playing to the crowd at the same time. A crowd that, by the way, was growing by the minute. It may have been the deprivation of being locked up for so long that had made him crave the attention.

By this time, the debacle had continued for almost an hour and the score was a shutout in the parrot's favor. The men were waiting for some opportunistic vendors to show up and take advantage of the large crowd that seemed to be enjoying this rare treat. They all knew we absorbed a portion of their tax dollars and now was a chance to see those dollars at work. Looking at the size of the gathering made me wish we had brought tickets to sell for the annual dance. I was also sure that by now a few members of our group were wishing we had a shotgun stowed away in one of the trucks to end this foolishness. Eventually, the commanders realized the parrot wasn't going to cooperate, so they cut their losses and sent us all back to the station.

A disappointed crowd was left wondering what would become of the poor parrot.

Only luck separated this incident from a house fire, in which the city's only ladder truck would be tied up trying to capture a wayward parrot. It certainly would have been a headline that would have been hard to live down. For many weeks afterwards, concerned citizens would inquire if the elusive bird was ever captured. "No," we would answer, "he was last seen heading west on Franklin Street." We could only hope time would bring more pertinent questions for us to answer.

What if we had been successful at capturing and relocating the runaway parrot, then what? Well, according to fire department tradition we would become the official parrot relocators, since precedent had been set. How else can you explain the bat removal service we extended to the city at that time? We had met with some success in the extrication of the disgusting little rodents from our citizens' homes, and by having some measure of success we had insured the continuation of this service. Now, I know bats have a purpose in God's plan and, really, I have nothing against them. Still, I have never been able to get too friendly with the alien-looking varmints, especially when it's up close and personal.

It was the typical bat in the house call. It wasn't as if we responded to these types of calls every day, but it certainly wasn't a first either. At the time, I was working at Engine 3 with "Fenway" Frank and Lt. Phil "Philly" Petrino. None of us could be considered a bat removal specialist, so we responded to the call somewhat lacking in enthusiasm.

Every time we answered a call like this, I'd wonder on the ride over, how the hell did it all ever get started? I mean, parrots, cats, bats, the names roll off the tongue easy enough, but who knows why the fire department is called to the scene?

Despite not being overly enthused, upon entering the house I tried to assume the best bat removal expert act that I could muster. Inside the house was a father and two teenage girls who were being held hostage by a lone vagrant bat. Naturally, this situation would elicit a call to the fire department for some help in evicting the hairy intruder and that's where we came in.

Now from past fire department lore, we had learned the best way to remove a bat was with a CO_2 fire extinguisher, which speaks highly as to the resourcefulness of prior members. How this method works is like this: the CO_2 is discharged with a blast of cold white moisture that freezes the bat, but only if it can be totally inundated in the icy cold smoke. In turn, the frozen rodent falls to the floor with a thud and is then removed from the premises. Amazingly, as it may seem, the bat soon thaws out and returns to its old rascally self and flies away.

So armed with a CO_2 extinguisher and some gloves, we entered the bedroom where the bat was spotted and closed the door behind us to block any chance of escape. The owner came in with us as well, apparently to lurk nearby and make critical comments whenever possible. He seemed to know exactly what needed to be done, only he needed three nitwits (I mean public servants) to execute the plan.

We decided a box or some such item was needed to put the bat into, if indeed we did make the proposed capture. Otherwise, we would risk the chance of the bat thawing out while in our gloved hands before exiting the house. This could lead to a loud shriek from a petrified firefighter and a bat being flung high in the air. The worst part of that scenario would be that the whole process would then need to be repeated, never mind the prospect of one us having a cardiac arrest. Besides, it would also badly tarnish our expert bat removal title. The idea of a bat suddenly flopping about in your hands was plenty of motivation to find a small secure container. After a brief search, Fenway found a small wicker basket with a nicely fitting cover and said, "It's empty except for this." As he held up in the air a piece of lacy material for us all to examine. We stopped to look at the basket, which was the perfect size, and then the lacy material that Fenway was holding up to the light trying to identify. Finally, realizing what he was holding up for examination was probably the sexiest piece of underwear that belonged to the man's wife, he dropped it to the ground and said, "Yeah, I'll just put these right here," as his face turned three shades of red. The man looked on with a slight grin and pretended he didn't notice.

Now with the basket in hand, there were no other reasons to delay any longer—it was time to try to capture the bat. In the bedroom, there were voluminous drapes surrounding the windows. The intruder was barely visible hiding inside one of the many folds. Fenway was holding the wicker basket, Philly was shining a hand light on the drapes and somehow I had ended up with the gloves on and the CO_2 canister. I should have gone for the basket but it was too late now, and Fenway seemed to have a really good grip on it. Carefully, I placed the nozzle of the canister near the bat and engulfed him in a huge blast of CO_2. Too much actually, but at this point I was a little trigger happy and figured better too much than too little. When the smoke cleared, the bat wasn't in the crease of the drape anymore, but he wasn't on the floor right below either. Cautiously, I poked at the drapes, but I still didn't see him. With concerned looks, we stood staring at the drapes, hoping maybe the bat had disappeared entirely like some magic trick. No such luck. After a moment, he crawled out from the shadows into the room. He didn't look too happy either. He seemed to be eyeing the lot of us with an angry expression. We backed up a bit in unison. Then up he flew, which sent us all ducking. He landed on the ceiling above us. I thought to myself, "Perhaps the bat has made a strategic mistake," since there was no cover nearby for him to hide behind.

Approaching from the rear in an attempt not to spook him, I gave him another strong dose of CO_2. This time he fell right to the floor, but he was only dazed and managed to crawl under the bed. Cautiously, Phil and I knelt down and peered under the bed. As I bent over, I inadvertently pulled the trigger of the CO_2 and blasted Philly right on the top of his head. He yelled and jumped up from the chill of the blast and I jumped up thinking the bat had done something to him. But upon seeing the CO_2 frost melting on his head, I realized it was not the bat, but yours truly who had done the damage. The citizen, the only witness present, was beginning to look at us with a quizzical frown. Obviously an opportunist, he chose this moment to question our ability to capture bats. With my most humble look, I offered him the gloves and the CO_2 container, asking him, "Would you like to give it a try?" He didn't answer, but somehow I sensed he would rather stand by doing nothing and just watch us with a look of quiet disapproval. Well, that wasn't going to get him anywhere. We had become immune to disapproving looks.

The bat, sensing the confusion and realizing we had forgotten all about him, seized the moment. He flew up in the air, which sent us all ducking towards the floor. This time he landed on top of the dresser mirror. Phil told me, "We don't have much CO_2 left, so make it good." We were running out of chances, but with renewed fervor I came forward, like a man on a mission. Holding the nozzle just a few inches away from the bat, I let him have it. He fell down behind the dresser like a brick, but was this some sort of ploy on his part? Rather than peek under the dresser we took no chances and moved the whole thing to inspect the area. There he was still stunned lying on the floor, but I gave him another good blast just to be sure he wasn't faking. Fenway brought the basket forward and with great trepidation, plus a few flinches, I hoisted him in and quickly put the lid on. It wasn't textbook, but he was in the basket and that's all we cared about.

The homeowner opened the door and announced to the two girls, "It's all right, we've got him!" The usage of the word *we* was definitely a stretch. I strutted out of the room like some knight returning from the Crusades, as Fenway asked the girls casually if they'd like to see the captured bat. They declined vigorously. He told them it was silly to be afraid, after all, it was only a little bat. We were three intrepid firefighters basking in the admiration of the girls. I was sure that their father would alter this perception immediately after our departure, but what the heck, we could enjoy our current status for the moment. Their father was less appreciative, but dared not say anything, since he claimed a share in the victory. Unless there had been a hidden camera in the room, our secret was safe.

After returning to the station, we placed the wicker basket outside on the walkway. Using a long pole, I knocked the basket over and the cover fell off the top. After a moment, a slightly disoriented bat ambled out on to the walk. Side by side, the three of us peered through the window at him. He seemed to do a brief flight check on all his equipment, then off he flew into the sky. I couldn't help wondering as he disappeared into the dusk that he might be returning to the house we just left.

A few days later, I told my brother, Dave, about our latest bat extrication and he told me with a grin, "In our city we don't do those anymore." "How did you manage that?" I asked. Well, it seemed as though one of the lieutenants on their department had inadvertently put an end to their entire bat removal service. The lieutenant was working a three-man engine crew that responded to a residential property to remove a bat from a citizen's living room. Upon arriving, he asked the woman who had called if she had a tennis racquet or something similar that he could borrow. After receiving the racquet, he told her, and the firefighter who accompanied him, to wait outside the living room and close the door behind him. After a few seconds of silence, there was a series of thuds and crashes from within the room. Growing concerned, the woman turned to the firefighter standing beside her and asked him, "What's he doing in there?" The firefighter, who was fairly new on the job, didn't have a clue so he told her not to worry because the lieutenant was a senior man and knew his business. Unfortunately, just like most firefighters his business was not bat removals.

After a few moments, things quieted down, the door opened and the lieutenant was standing there dangling a lifeless bat by the wing. He handed it to the firefighter and told him, "Take it out and put it in front of one of the truck's wheels and we'll run it over as we leave just to be sure it's dead." Then he turned to the woman and said, "You're all set, ma'am." And without another word, he headed back to the pump. Flabbergasted, the woman watched him walk out of the house and then looked inside the living room. Well, let's just say some of the contents had been slightly rearranged. Evidently, a call was immediately made to headquarters to share this information and, to say the least, it wasn't a thank you.

The next day, the dispatch office received a written note that said, "No fire personnel will respond to any bat removal calls until further notice." In one fell swoop, this lieutenant had managed to put an end to the ridiculous bat removal service that the city had been providing. Unfortunately, the city I worked in still offered it, but if we ever really wanted to get out of the business, at least now we knew how.

An Honest Mistake

I N MY YOUNGER DAYS, I was resistant to influence or advice from anyone without the highest credentials. It would be like trying to pour water into a stone, my head was that hard. But I had a strong capacity to learn especially when the lesson left a scar.

We were in the first day of our four-day cycle. I was working on the rescue as part of a two-man crew with another EMT (emergency medical technician). My partner enjoyed the medical end of our profession and was on his way to earning a degree in nursing at night school. It required a lot of shift swapping because of our rotating schedule, but his perseverance and natural aptitude for studying had helped him along. Now he knew the Latin derivatives for most of the words I couldn't even pronounce and he was becoming quite a nuisance with his newly acquired knowledge. He looked the part as well, with his round-rimmed glasses and his penchant for collegiate sweaters.

None of this was missed by our fellow firefighters, who were referring to him as a nurse or doctor instead of a rescue man. He would have preferred professor, but that wasn't going to happen. Yet, I must admit, on rescue calls it was nice to have a walking medical textbook on the scene. He was always more than willing to share his knowledge with those who dwell in ignorance, which is where I usually resided when intricate medical knowledge was discussed. This reduced my role on most calls to that of a willing assistant or an excellent gopher. Yet, I prided myself on hustling at the emergency calls. After all, time is one of the few variables that can be altered to produce some benefit in the outcome of an emergency call. So I may have been a gopher, but at least I was a first-class one. In fact, my specialty was removing people with back injuries who needed to be carried down a flight of stairs. Being a mover (my side job) gave me the unique experience of moving fragile and heavy objects with as little jarring as possible. I guess I was a gopher with a specialty. Despite our discrepancy in talent, neither one of us were physicians, but you tried hard to do a tough job and said a little prayer for good measure.

I don't remember what I was doing when the voice came over the loud speaker, but it was a call for the rescue company to respond to a residential address for a woman having difficulty breathing. I was riding in the jump seat that day and my partner was driving. He loved to drive but wasn't especially good at it, so I arrived at every call a little bit on edge. We took pride in responding to any part of the city in just a few minutes, and this call was no different. Some people were amazed at how fast we arrived, although others complained we had taken forever. I suppose it depended on your frame of mind at the time. The passage of time must be impossible to measure by normal standards when you're bleeding or gasping for air.

We arrived at a single family house in a shade under three minutes. My partner carried in the jump kit and I ran around to a side compartment to get our portable oxygen and followed him into the house. When I entered he was attending a woman in her late thirties who was sitting in a chair. By her side stood a younger woman who looked visibly shaken. The medical wizard told me to get a simple face mask with four to six liters of oxygen on the patient, even though this was standard operating procedure and I would have done it anyway. He went about getting all the vital information while I set up the oxygen. It was apparent we would be transporting the woman to the hospital, so I went for the cot and readied it next to the patient. It was an easy exit from the house to the rescue truck. Basically a straight shot, with just a couple of stairs. The rule of thumb was if you suspected the patient might have a heart condition, then you carried them to the truck, although some people didn't like being carried if they felt they could walk (especially if the neighbors were watching). We always told patients that we would get in trouble if we were to let them walk, so they'd get on the cot for our sake, instead of theirs.

As he took her blood pressure, I was idle for a moment and now free to take a better look around. We had learned that the two were mother and daughter, yet they almost looked like sisters. Both had black hair, dark eyes, olive skin and a definite family resemblance was apparent, even to a total stranger.

The mother was trying to remain calm for her daughter's sake, but she was in obvious distress. The daughter was doing the same, though a tremble in their hands betrayed the both of them. We strapped our patient on to the cot and prepared her for transport. She was giving her daughter instructions on what to do after we left: her father must be called; the food in the oven must be shut off; the front door was to be left unlocked for her brother, and so on. The daughter asked her what she might need at the hospital: a house-coat, flat shoes, make-up, her pocketbook? We hated to break up the conversation but our patient was having trouble breathing. It was obvious being separate was not what either of them wanted at that moment. To get things going, we told the daughter to meet us at the emergency room as soon as she completed all of her mother's requests. You always feel better when the patient is loaded in the truck and you're en route. The hospital was only minutes away and that meant doctors, nurses and all the marvels of modern medicine. Unlike the movies in which someone can say, "scene one, take two," in the real world there are no second chances.

As we began the drive to the hospital, I called ahead informing them of our ETA, the patient's vital signs and other pertinent information we had obtained. We were underway no more than a half minute when I heard my partner call the woman by name. I glanced in the mirror to see what was going on in the back of the rescue. My partner was trying to get a response from the woman. He was checking her pulse with one hand and tapping her cheek with the other. Once again, he called her name and there was still no response. This struck me as odd since she had been talking only a few seconds ago. I asked if I should call an engine to the scene and come back to help him with our patient. He told me she had a strong pulse and to continue on to the hospital. Sensing this call might be going downhill, I dropped the hammer to the gas pedal and put the siren on full time.

Our destination was no more than a minute and a half ahead. Now traveling faster, I could only occasionally glance in the mirror to see what was happening in the back. It was obvious there was no sign of a response and I could detect some nervousness in my partner's voice. I asked if he was making any progress. This time the answer was just a terse "No!" It was with a feeling of relief that I made the last turn for the emergency room entrance of the hospital.

There was plenty of help at the ER that day and they were outside waiting for us. I parked in one of the bays and rushed around to help unload our patient. My partner explained to a waiting staff member how our patient had suddenly lapsed into unconsciousness, but remarked that her pulse remained strong. After reaching the trauma room, the staff did a quick survey and decided our patient was in respiratory arrest and began to manually breathe her with an Ambu Bag. We had been supplying her with oxygen that she hadn't been breathing. My partner stood there stunned at this turn of events. He turned and looked at me, and I'm sure I looked just as stunned as he did.

They started to cut off her clothing and attach the electrodes that might be necessary to try to shock her back to life. They started to intubate her airway to help make the manual breathing more effective. There is no such thing as dignity when you're on a cot in the trauma room. Her body was limp and pale, no longer resembling the woman we first saw, but instead a lifeless mannequin was in her place. To see life leave a body is a grotesque thing. I silently asked God to help this woman and hoped to see some improvement. None seemed to come. I began to feel out of place standing there among the hospital staff, so I took the empty cot and went out into the hall to get new linens.

As I stood there dressing the cot, my mind retraced the call from the beginning to the end. She had lapsed into unconsciousness without complaint or even a sound for that matter. Suddenly, behind me a voice asked, "How's my mother doing?" I turned and looked right into the eyes of her daughter. My heart pounded and my insides churned as I looked into her unknowing face. I had forgotten she was supposed to meet us here. What was

I going to tell her? I selfishly thought to myself, "Why did I have to be standing here? I'm a firefighter not a doctor." She sensed something was wrong immediately. I said to myself, "Don't be a coward, just do the best you can." This was one situation we were never trained for in EMT school. Taking hold of her hand, I told her that her mother had taken a turn for the worse but the emergency room staff were doing everything they could. For a minute, I thought that she would faint, so I helped her to a waiting room chair and then sat next to her still holding her hand. I felt her grip tighten as the tears began to fill her eyes. It felt so intrusive being there at such a private moment, but her grip told me she didn't want me to leave. I sat quietly at her side. There were absolutely no words I could think of that would sound anything but hollow, so I just patted her shoulder and held her trembling hand. She began to sob and I hoped that by some miracle, word would come that her mother was improving. None came. None would come that day. Her mother would pass away a short time later.

After a while, another family member arrived on the scene. He came to her side and began to console her. I patted her hand one last time and got up to leave. She looked at me and mouthed the words "Thank you." I felt so guilty as I turned to walk away, tears now burned in my eyes as well. My heart was breaking for her. I finished preparing the cot and loaded it on the rescue. My partner was already out there putting the oxygen away. We drove back to the station in silence, each of us lost in our own thoughts.

Later at the station, we discussed every aspect of the call at length. Just the two of us sitting in the back room of the firehouse at two in the morning. I told him I had never seen respiratory arrest before without cardiac arrest and the fact that she had a good pulse probably would have fooled me, too. He said he had seen it before, but never as subtle or as quick as today. We decided she was without oxygen for less than two minutes, which usually wasn't enough to kill someone, but nothing seemed to absolve us from the guilt we were feeling.

What I didn't hear that night were any Latin phrases or medical jargon. My partner was totally humbled by the experience, and no explanations would make either of us feel any better. The only thing that seemed to help in these situations was a poor man's therapy: one too many drinks and the passage of time. Just sitting alone at home, at times in the middle of the night, nursing a drink and trying to deal with feelings that remained unresolved. Sometimes, it helped to talk to another firefighter, one who had been through similar situations. Maybe it felt better just to hear someone say you're not the only one who ever made a mistake, and know the person saying it had stood in the same shoes as you. Eventually, I think every firefighter learns that depression is just a job-related injury.

Our normal training provided us with only an eighty-one-hour course in basic emergency medicine. You might think that our minimal training would preclude feelings of guilt when an erroneous medical decision was made, but it doesn't. I'll remember a mother who passed away that day and a daughter with a hopeful expression looking into my eyes. I'll probably remember it the rest of my life. Since then I've learned not every call turns out the way you want it to, but still, the feelings of regret and guilt cannot be erased.

———————————

(Emergency medicine is a tricky business. It's only two words, but it covers every combination of medical needs that you can possibly imagine. An emergency can be chaotic even in the hospital, but that pales in comparison to emergencies handled out in the streets. The greater the knowledge and tools at your disposal, the greater the success you'll have when every minute counts. Many rescue trucks and ambulances are now requiring at least one paramedic to be in attendance when answering emergency calls. Their training is vastly superior to that of a basic EMT. I'm not saying mistakes or oversights won't still happen, only that it's hard to even call it a *mistake* when people with so little training are asked to do so much.)

THE LAUGHING LIEUTENANT

S ITTING ON A CHAIR with his upper body sprawled across a kitchen table was a young man who appeared to be about nineteen years old. He was unconscious and the surface of the table was completely covered with his blood. Standing close by were his two younger sisters who were fairly close in age, evidently one of them had made the call that summoned us to the scene.

Richard Fink and I were working on the rescue that night. The call over the loudspeaker had been for "a man down." It would have been nice going out the door to know why he was down, but some of the dispatchers seemed determined to give out as little information as possible. Man down from a heart problem, gunshot wound, a fall off a roof, whatever, at least give us something to think about on the ride to the scene. Can you imagine the difference between answering a call and finding someone "down" from a dizzy spell as opposed to someone "down" from an explosion?

As I walked around the table to examine the victim I slipped and lost my balance for a second. When I reached out to steady myself, I knocked over a container on the kitchen counter. The reason for my slip was another large pool of blood on the floor beneath my feet. On this job, you learn that blood is slippery, in fact, on a linoleum floor like the one in that kitchen, it's almost as slick as motor oil. One of the girls said to her brother, "John, the firefighters are here. John, they're here!" She said it as if her brother was pretending to be unaware of our presence. While I attempted to get a pulse, Rich asked her what had happened. The elder of the two did all the talking because the younger one seemed too embarrassed. She told him John had forgot his key, so he punched out a small pane of glass in order to unlock the front door and in the process sliced his arm open. It didn't take a wizard to surmise that their parents were away for the night and brother John had taken advantage of the situation by coming home stinking drunk, probably long after he was expected.

By this time, we had determined the boy had a pulse, but not much of one. As Rich walked over to open up our jump kit for supplies he slipped and fell against a wall. We were beginning to look more like a vaudeville act rather than a rescue company. The two girls couldn't help but giggle at the performance of our floor show, the gravity of the scene that confronted us hadn't seemed to register with them at all.

After he regained his footing, Rich grabbed a gauze dressing and some sterile water, it was time to take a look at the wound. One arm hung idly next to the boy's side, while the bleeding arm was lying on the table next to his head, bent at the elbow. As I straightened the arm to take a look at the wound a stream blood shot through the air. Quickly, I folded it back up and asked Rich for the gauze dressing. From the quick peek we had of the damage, it looked as though he had sliced his arm open just above the elbow, near the brachial artery. The girls were so preoccupied in a quiet animated conversation that they didn't see the geyser, as far as they were concerned, brother John was just putting on a show.

When I straightened the arm again, Rich applied the gauze with some direct pressure, but this time the blood only oozed out. While he finished dressing the wound, I quickly ran out and retrieved our cot for transport. By the time I had the cot ready for the patient, Rich had the wound dressed and the portable oxygen hooked up. He asked me if we should get any more vitals before we moved the victim. "No," I replied. "Let's get him in the rescue and start traveling, anything else we'll get on the way." Time seemed like the most important issue, as I looked around at the amount of blood in the room. The two girls giggled and shook their heads, to think that their brother would actually make us pick him up and place him on the cot. "How far was he going to take this thing?" you could almost hear them thinking. The eldest sister had her driver's license even though she looked as if she was about fourteen. She would take her brother's car and the two of them would meet us at the hospital. The thought of driving to the hospital in the middle of the night had the two of them positively giddy with excitement.

Everything was done very quickly from this point on, there was no time to lose. His weak pulse and pale coloring were obvious signs that his circulatory system was failing. As we sped towards the hospital, I stared at his chest to make sure that he was still breathing, and pressed hard into his wrists with my fingers to detect his barely palpable pulse. About halfway to the hospital, I was beginning to think we would need to start CPR (cardiopulmonary resuscitation), when suddenly John began talking inaudibly and moving as if half awake. I grabbed him under the chin, trying to keep him conscious saying, "Breathe in the oxygen, John, and try to stay awake." What he needed badly was an IV and that was something we weren't capable of providing. Just give us sixty more seconds, I thought to myself, and we'll have you at the doors of the emergency room. About a block from the hospital, he lapsed back into unconsciousness, but we weren't going to begin CPR a hundred yards from our destination. Besides, the flame had flared up once before when I thought the candle was out.

Rich had radioed the emergency room and made them aware of our patient's situation, so they would be ready for us when we backed into their bay. I couldn't move fast enough because this kid was as close to the next world as you can get. "God, it would be awful to see a young man this age die!" I thought as we unloaded the cot and wheeled him into the hospital. The ER staff went to work as soon as we transferred our patient to a hospital gurney. They quickly hooked him up to an IV and started pumping in some fluids. As I looked at his deathly pale coloring, I could feel my own heart pounding from the pressure of the scene. Rich and I watched anxiously as the pros worked on the poor kid, the seconds seemed like minutes to us. Then, the IV must have kicked in because John started to stir. He was like Lazarus coming back from the dead, you could almost see traces of color return to his cheeks. The two of us glanced at each other with unspoken "Thank God" looks of relief. We had definitely dodged an emotional bullet.

We headed back out into the corridor feeling better than when we whisked our patient through it a few minutes earlier. After every call, the linens on the cot needed to be changed and the rescue restocked to replace any supplies that were used. It was a common practice at the time for the hospital receiving our patient to replace whatever supplies were used and also provide us with fresh linens. As we wheeled the cot back to the rescue, I could see the two sisters sitting in the waiting room. "Is he ready to go home yet?" the eldest one asked. "No, it will probably be a little while, but one of the emergency room staff will be able to give you a better idea," I answered matter of factly. There was no sense in alarming them, now that the crisis was over. The two girls shook their heads and rolled their eyes at my answer. "How long will this charade go on?" they were probably thinking. When we got back into the rescue Rich looked over at me for a long second and said, "They really don't understand how serious an injury that was, do they?"

"Not a clue!" I replied and we both laughed ironically, as firefighters sometimes do after a bad situation turns out okay.

It was only because of an overtime that we worked together that night, Rich was a member of Group 1. I was assigned to Group 4. Although the two of us were stationed at headquarters, we usually only saw each other in passing, maybe exchanging a word or two.

Each group at the firehouse has its own unique combination of personalities. On the whole all the groups are quite similar, but each station, or even each piece, for that matter, will have its own subtle differences. For myself, the ideal situation would be working with good firefighters who also try to have some fun around the station. People who respect your space, but at the same time make the most of a workday. After all, this is a big part of your life and the thousands of hours spent at the firehouse can fall anywhere on that proverbial scale of one through ten.

On the low end of the scale, there are one punch knockouts and wrestling matches. On the other end, there can be side-splitting laughter or a Sunday brunch to enjoy, before watching our favorite football game. Obviously, the difference between these two extremes can mean everything in terms of the quality of your working life. Most of my workdays fell somewhere in the middle of the spectrum, but that never prevented me from striving to achieve that elusive ten on the scale.

On that lower end, sometimes things get a little weird. Tensions can run pretty high when clashing personalities are confined to the same space for long periods of time. Intolerance of another individuals' idiosyncrasies can cause conflicts over petty differences. Yes, at times the firehouse was like a powder keg and the smallest spark could set off an explosion. For instance, "If that animal sleeping in the rack next to me farts one more time, I'll put that human gas machine out of service for good. I mean what the hell is this a zoo?" Or "If that nitwit touches the remote again, I'll introduce him to the naked stranglehold until he stops moving!" Or how about, "If I open the refrigerator and my milk is gone again, I'll break into the locker of the group that worked the last shift and urinate all over their entire stock of dry goods!"

Now this might sound like hyperbole to an outsider, but I've seen events such as this take place and, sadly enough, have participated in a few as well. Here is a quick true story to prove the point. It involves three individuals, Gabby, Grouchy and the Bystander, who were together in the day room at the beginning of a night shift, which I know sounds like an oxymoron.

The first party of this trio was a talker, I mean a real talker. He could talk at thirty miles an hour with gusts up to sixty, without breaking a sweat. The second party of the group sometimes arrived for the night shift with, shall we say, less than a rosy disposition. The third party, an innocent bystander really, was just trying to read the daily newspaper. Well, the talker arrived for this particular shift wound up tighter than a mainspring, even more so than usual, and began a long-winded narration of the events of his day. After listening to him for awhile Grouchy started eyeballing him like a pit bull does a neighbor's poodle. The newspaper reader just ignored most of the verbal barrage, but would nod his head occasionally just to be polite. Grouchy finally told Gabby, "Why don't you give your mouth a rest before you pass out from lack of oxygen!" But Gabby was so wrapped up in his rambling monologue that he barely acknowledged Grouchy's protest. The Bystander just smiled nodding his head once again.

By this time, daggers were shooting out of Grouchy's eyes, but Gabby didn't even seem to notice. Suddenly without warning, Grouchy jumped up and grabbed Gabby by the throat shouting, "Will you shut the hell up?" Gabby, who was a smaller man, would have liked to say, "Okay!" But Grouchy's grip was so strong he couldn't even get the words out, besides with all of his talking there wasn't much air left in his lungs anyway. The newspaper reader peeked over his paper and saw that Gabby was now turning beet red and glassy eyed, which provoked him into yelling, "Grouchy, for God's sake let him go before you kill him!" But Grouchy wasn't responding. By now, he had a glazed look in his eyes and his grip didn't loosen, even as Gabby fell to his knees. Again the Bystander yelled, "Let him go!" But it was too late for words now, Grouchy was over the edge and wouldn't respond to anything. Finally, not knowing what to do, the Bystander went over and unleashed a major right hand to Grouchy's head, knocking him cold on the spot. A few of the firefighters in the television room, who had heard the commotion, came out to take a look and see what was going on. What they saw was the Bystander leaving with a newspaper tucked under his arm and a disgusted look on his face, Grouchy sprawled on the day room floor unconscious and Gabby down on all fours panting like a dog on a hot day.

This is a classic example of a one on the previously mentioned scale, and it can make for a long shift. (By the way, no charges were ever filed on this incident, afterwards it was just business as usual.) Now, a situation like that is not an everyday occurrence, but these things do happen. On the other hand, a tour of duty at the station can be a ball. Grilling steaks on the barbecue while trying to decide which lottery numbers to play for the night. Ordering a pay-per-view championship fight and having Chinese food delivered for the occasion. Getting a little weird and playing strip ping-pong, until some poor fellow wanders in looking for directions and you realize either you better lock the front door or stop playing strip ping-pong. Playing combat golf with ping-pong balls, where each direct hit on a fellow firefighter is a point in your favor. It's like being back in high school again and driving the teachers crazy, until the bells ring and then you get serious. Your classic ten would be when it seemed like a shift ended too quickly because the time just flew by, so you actually hang around a little while before heading home. The point is the right combination of personalities at the station can make all the difference in the world.

When I transferred to Engine 3, I lost contact with some of the members on our fire department. At the time Engine 3 ran a pump manned by three firefighters, previously I had worked at headquarters, which had a pump, a ladder truck and a rescue, so there had been more firefighters around on a daily basis. Engine 3 also responded to fewer calls as well, so due to the nature of our running assignments I had less contact with the rest of the department. There were a few fire alarm activations to which all the apparatus responded, but outside of those alarm assignments my contact with some individuals was greatly diminished. In certain cases that really wasn't a bad thing, but there were individuals whom I really had enjoyed working with and I missed seeing them on a regular basis. Yet, it was by my own bid that I was stationed at Engine 3, so it was my choice and I really couldn't complain.

By negotiating with the chief and the city, the union had been able to obtain the bidding process, which was a real plum for the fire department. Before that time, job assignments had been completely controlled by the captains or the chief, and the results could be unfair. Oftentimes, assignments had been given out according to personalities or favoritism, and seniority was given little, or no, consideration at all. It had reached the point where most of the members of the department would say, "Seniority didn't mean jack squat!" Now, I don't exactly know Webster's definition of *jack squat*, but I do know that in firehouse vernacular, it wasn't good. So by virtue of the union's tireless efforts, I had secured a permanent berth at Engine 3 with a bid.

Why Engine 3? Well, for one thing I didn't have enough seniority to get to Engine 2, which seemed to be the most coveted station at which to work. Engine 3 had a nice gym and did a lot less runs than headquarters and it also put considerable distance between myself and city hall. Headquarters sat exactly adjacent to city hall and that always seemed to be a source of controversy or rumor mongering. Besides, the atmosphere at the outside stations always seemed more relaxed and since my clock was always wound a little too tight anyway, it was definitely a good thing for me.

Engine 3 ran with a bare bones crew, so if one of us were to be out injured for any length of time, another person would need to be transferred over until the regular crew member was ready to return to duty. This was the case when Richard Fink was transferred over to Group 4 at Engine 3 to fill in at the lieutenant position. Rich would be filling in for Phil Petrino who was out with a shoulder injury. When they realized that Phil needed an operation they didn't bother calling overtime to cover his spot, instead they transferred a junior lieutenant to cover the spot until Phil was recovered and ready to return to work. We all had complete confidence that Phil would eventually be back since he was no stranger to injuries and operations. In the time that I worked with Phil Petrino he had his wrist, knee, shoulder and back operated on, and each time he struggled through the pain and therapy to return to the job. The cynics would have you believe that every city employee's dream is to be injured on the job so they can collect disability and never return to work, but time and time again I've witnessed firefighters struggle to return to a job that they really love.

Rich Fink had gone through EMT school at the same time as me and we had responded to a few calls together, the most memorable one I described earlier. Yet in almost ten years on the job, we had never served on the same piece for more than a day. As a youngster, I always thought my life was so unique, my problems or aspirations were unlike anyone else's, but after being on the fire department for a while I realized that wasn't the case and Ritchie was a good example. We were both the same age, we had both served in the military, Ritchie was married and had two children, the eldest a boy, the youngest a girl. My situation was exactly the same, in fact, we both even had a dog as well. We were two regular guys working at the fire department and also working a side job to supplement our income. It's one of life's humbling truths to realize you're not special, well, at least no more than anyone else.

So it would be Rich Fink as the lieutenant and Fenway Frank and myself as the firefighters on Engine 3, at least until

Phil recovered from his injury and returned to his normal slot. We spent the first week getting to know one another, getting familiar with each others idiosyncrasies—of course, the other fellow's quirks are always worse than yours. Ritchie was definitely easy to be around, with his laid-back personality. On the other hand, my pins seem to get knocked over way too easy, so if an individual wished to pick an argument I definitely could be provoked. Now, with Phil I never had a problem, because arguing with Phil would be like arguing with myself. We agreed on almost everything, whether it was politics, religion or how the world rotated on its axis and it didn't take long to realize I wouldn't have a problem with Ritchie either. Ritchie would always agree to disagree before voices got raised, that was just his nature.

During the next few weeks, we found our rhythm while answering all the uneventful routine calls that a normal firefighting work week can bring. The combination was working, Ritchie was definitely a good firefighter. The job was important to him, when we went out the door he always tried to make sure upon returning we had done our best. In one small way, we did differ quite a bit, though. Whenever we arrived on a scene he'd pause for a moment to think about what he was going to do. Not the normal pause that everybody takes, especially if you're in charge. No, I'm talking about an elongated pause, an unusually long pause, and for me with my nature, this was agony. I was always all adrenaline—let's go, let's do it—but whenever I asked Rich, "What do you want to do?" all of a sudden he'd go into that pause mode, as if he had a delayed fuse in his head. Then, after what seemed like an eternity to me, he'd say, "Okay, this is what we're going to do," and it was good firefighting. So each time we reached a scene, he'd pause to consider the circumstances— whether he had all the bases covered and so forth—while I would do this silent dance next to him, raring to go but trying to avoid getting my underwear in a knot. When you work a three-man engine company, it's important to have a trio that works well together. You don't want three hard chargers or three deep thinkers, nor do you want three jokesters or three deep sleepers. If the other firefighter's strength is your weakness, a certain balance is achieved, and in firefighting that's a plus.

Around the engine house, Ritchie was a recliner potato. When we weren't busy, he'd be in a recliner with a magazine or newspaper, or playing with his mustache as he watched television. The image of him sitting there became so familiar that, to this day, I can picture it in my mind with no problem at all. Fenway Frank would be in his room sorting baseball cards for his card shop and I might be in my room, reading a book or checking my eyelids for leaks, while Rich was stretched out in that recliner. This was the exact setting the first time we heard the famous Rich Fink funny bone get tickled.

The sound of Ritchie giggling at something on television drifted into our rooms. Soon the giggles turned to laughter, then the laughter jumped up an octave to a higher pitch. Well, the lieutenant found something good to watch on TV, I thought to myself. He laughed and laughed, before the room finally went silent, but then after a few seconds there was the sound of hysterical laughter—he had only been silent for that moment because he was having trouble catching his breath. His laughter had only shifted gears. It went from a sporadic chuckle to a full belly laugh and then disappeared into a high-pitched hee, hee, hee. Fenway poked his head into my room and said, "I'm going to check this out, whatever he's watching must be pretty good." Soon there was a duet of laughter ringing in my ears, accompanied by the occasional knee slap. Now, there aren't many movies that make me laugh, but it wasn't long before I had to go out and see what the hell was so funny. As it turned out, Frank and I had both already seen what Ritchie was watching and we had only found it slightly amusing, but that was without Rich present. Ritchie and his infectious laugh made all the difference in the world, now the same movie was nothing short of hysterical. We were all having a good laugh when the loudspeaker interrupted our merriment for an alarm sounding in a building. It was a nothing call, but by the time we got back the movie was over and it was back to the book I had been reading, which now seemed a little boring.

On our first night shift, Frank found the same movie that we had been watching the previous day listed in the television guide, so we flipped it on and before long we were all hysterical with laughter again. This was amazing to me. A movie that I barely found amusing the first time, I was now watching for the third time and laughing until my ribs ached, because of Ritchie. I really didn't understand how that worked, but it didn't change the fact that I was having a ball. By the end of the movie, I needed a break anyway, I hadn't laughed that much in ten years.

When our second night rolled around, Fenway began the shift by scanning the television guide for comedies. It was obvious that he was hoping for another laugh fest, but what he found wasn't really Ritchie's type of comedy. It didn't elicit anything but a few giggles from him, and amazingly, if he didn't laugh, we didn't laugh either. A new approach was needed. Something this good couldn't be left to chance so we asked Rich who his favorite comedians were and Rich gave us a rundown. A liberal rundown I might add, because he does have a rather large funny bone. Despite the knowledge of what tickled him, we couldn't come up with a single thing on the countless cable channels at our disposal, so all we could do was hope for better luck the next time we worked.

It might sound crazy, but I was already growing addicted to this laughter. Those few sessions of group laughter had managed to unwind my clock a couple of ticks and it felt good. This was medicinal—it was for my health, it was brain balm. I had stumbled into some kind of weird therapy and I needed it. So on my off-duty days I decided that the situation really couldn't be left to chance, it was off to the video store to rent one of the comedies Ritchie had mentioned. I saved it for the night shift because on the days we were often running around too much to sit and watch a movie. Fenway thought it was a great idea, and as far as Rich knew I was just a good Samaritan, he had no clue of his vital role in the entertainment. Rich had said he liked the movie and he certainly didn't let us down. Fenway and I were once again swept away in a tide of humor—unconstrained laughter ensued. The idea of renting a movie worked beautifully, because if we had to respond to a call during the film we simply hit the stop button on the way out the door, then upon returning we could hit the play button when we were ready and, bingo, in ten minutes we were laughing again.

My wife, Joan, asked me after a few movie rentals, "Why, all of a sudden, this interest in these comedies you're bringing to work?"

"You have to hear him laugh," I told her.

She smiled and thought it was funny, but she really didn't understand. If she had been in the room with us during one of these productions, I'm sure she would have been laughing just as hard as the three of us, and probably wouldn't know why either.

By now, this laughter really was becoming a drug. I was spending money every week as if I needed a fix for my funny bone.

Each week, I was bringing in a movie for our night shifts and sometimes, if the video store was running a special, I'd bring in a back-up just to play it safe. Rich seemed to have an endless capacity for laughter while Frank and I went to this well of humor as often as we could.

Phil's finally back, he's indestructible! The bionic man had endured another operation and still he returned to a job, which at times, could be very physically demanding. We had worked together a long time, but I wished it was a four-man engine company so we could keep Ritchie around. I told him it had been a pleasure working with him, and hopefully we would do it again soon, although because of our schedules it wasn't likely. Ritchie ended up working on my own shift, but at Engine 2, so it would be almost impossible for us to work together. Anyone filling in for vacations or sickness would be from another shift. I hoped the firefighters who worked with Ritchie appreciated that infectious laugh because, if not, what a waste. You'd need to have a face like a closed fist to not crack a smile at that famous Rich Fink laugh. I hoped somewhere down the road I'd have another chance to experience it.

Early one morning a few years later, we were awakened to a call over the loudspeaker for a house fire on West Emerson Street. It was out of our district so we turned on the scanner to hear the report from the first engine to arrive at the scene. If we were lucky, it might not be much so we could hit the hay again and grab a little more sleep, before the day crew arrived. The first voice we heard was that of Rich Fink in Engine 2 reporting, "Heavy smoke showing." Within a few seconds, we were dispatched to the scene. The lieutenant told me on the way to the scene that we would be laying a line to the fire. My job, as the firefighter operating out of the jump seat, was to dress a hydrant that would be used as a water supply. Engine 3 stopped just long enough for me to wrap the hydrant with a line and grab our tool bucket, then it proceeded down the street to the fire. As it did, length after length of line was pulled from the hose bed. A single wrap of line around the hydrant secured by the heel of my foot kept hydrant connection from being dragged down the street behind the engine. Making a hydrant is probably the most basic job in firefighting, but what it provides is of the utmost importance and nothing can be taken for granted. Every once in a while, you will run into a bad hydrant and you can't wait too long to find that out, so I quickly dressed the hydrant and tested it to make sure it was working.

As I waited for the pump operator's call for water, I had a chance to eyeball the house. It was one of the huge Victorians (which the city of Melrose has a generous portion of) and if it really got going it would be a tough stop. After they called for water, I charged the line and completed my job at the hydrant. I always got antsy waiting because all the real action is right down the street in front of you, but if you ever send the water before they're ready somebody can get seriously hurt at the other end. A brass coupling at the end of a hose line whipping through the air, at what seems like the speed of light, will do some serious damage to the human body. Now all I needed was to don an airtank and grab an ax—more manpower was certainly needed in the building.

Someone in the crowd of bystanders had told the captain that a young man rented a room on the third floor and that he was unaccounted for at this point. The Engine 2 company was in the process of doing a sweep of the third floor to make sure there wasn't a possible victim who had been overcome by smoke. I brought up a hand line to back them up. On the second floor,

I could hear the firefighters on the floor above shouting as they searched the room hoping for a response if someone was still there. At this time, we had no thermal imaging equipment, so the firefighters had to physically sweep the room to make sure there was no one unconscious in some remote corner. Even in a normal size room, blinding smoke can make the task very difficult since you're in such alien territory. Is this a window or a door? Is there a second exit to the room? Did we search every closet? Someone's life could depend on it and to leave a job half done is inviting tragedy.

At the foot of the stairs to the third floor, stood Rich Fink, he was keeping tabs on his crew who were conducting the search. Next to him was a wall that he had opened up and there was fire showing in the breach. Since we had a line handy, I opened it up and gave the area a good dousing, but almost immediately after shutting down the line for a quick look, it lit right up again. Ritchie looked at me and said, "I've hit that area with a line a few times, Doug, but it just keeps lighting back up." Usually that meant the source of the problem was somewhere else, most likely extending upwards from somewhere below. I really didn't have anything else to do at that moment but back up the Engine 2 crew, so I decided to open up the wall a little more with my pick-ax and try to put the water to better use, but no matter how much water I poured into that opening the fire just kept coming back.

It wasn't long before we noticed that the smoke conditions were steadily deteriorating and it wasn't only coming from the wall we had opened up. The Engine 2 crew descended from the third floor and said the upstairs was clear. The low-air warning bells on their tanks were ringing so it was time for them to exit the building, leaving only Rich and I on the second floor.

We would find out later that the young man that slept on that third floor was outside standing in the crowd watching the fire like everyone else. He didn't know that firefighters were crawling around a smoke-filled room on the third floor looking for him, while a fire growing out of control burned beneath them. This is always a problem at house fires: reports of missing tenants, when outside of the structure the fire scene hasn't even been checked. Someone in charge at the scene hadn't taken enough time to confirm that a resident wasn't actually missing and firefighters were taking risks on what really was just hearsay.

We lingered a moment after the other firefighters departed, then suddenly Ritchie said loudly, "I'm out of air."

"Ya, my (low-air) bell's ringing, too," I replied thinking that he meant it was time to exit the building.

"No, I mean I'm out!" He replied with a sense of urgency.

With all the protective gear you have on inside of a burning building, sometimes you forget just how hazardous the atmosphere surrounding you actually is—we were about to find out. Rich stepped over to a window that had been punched out and tried to grab some fresh air. It was so smoky by this time I didn't realize that there was only a small opening in the window and it was edged with jagged broken glass. As I went over to see if I could help him, he bolted towards the stairs. I thought he had grabbed some badly needed air and now he was headed out. Following him towards the exit, I could sense from his body language that a sense of desperation was setting in and he was beginning to panic.

As we headed towards the stairs that led outside, I discarded my ax and tried to loosen my mask so I could share what was left of my air with him. While I was momentarily distracted by this, I heard him yell, "Oh, Jesus Christ!" as he turned into a side room away from the stairs that led to the safety outside the house. The sound of those three words sent a chill down my spine and left no doubt of how desperate things were becoming. Within seconds, I heard a crashing noise come from inside the room he had entered, as Rich tried in vain to find an exit. There was no time left to waste. I could see nothing in the room because the smoke was so thick. Instead of screwing with my helmet and gloves while removing my own mask I merely tossed them to the floor. Then holding my mask to my face I entered the room to try to get Rich the hell out of there. I realized one thing was in our favor after removing my helmet and gloves, the temperature in the building hadn't reached lung incinerating levels yet—thank God! Rich was easy to find despite being blinded by the smoke. His frantic attempts at finding an exit were loud enough to lead me right to him. I attempted to verbally give him an idea of how we could get out of there, but he was beyond being rational. So with all the force I could muster, I grabbed him by the shoulder of his jacket and immobilized him. Then I thrust my mask on to his face and held it there for a second, telling him to stay still for a moment and just breathe through the mask. The feeling of fresh air had an immediate calming effect on him—it must have been as welcomed as a life ring to a drowning man. Then forcefully I said, "Rich, we're going to walk out of this room to the staircase and get out of here." He couldn't help but follow that air mask as the two of us walked out of the room towards the stairs. When we reached a point where the front door was visible I asked him if he was all right. He gave me a thumbs up, took a deep breath and went down the rest of the stairs. I watched him go until he was out of the building.

It was a relief to know he was safe outside, but before I left there was something I had to do. Every retired firefighter has an old helmet somewhere that bears the scars of his career, mine was upstairs lying on the hall floor somewhere and I wanted it back. I tried to put my air mask on but that last gulp of air by Rich must have finished what was left. Well, it wasn't too far, I thought to myself, so I headed back up to the top of the stairs for a quick retrieve. Easier said than done. The same smoke that disoriented Rich was now choking me and the visibility was almost down to zero. I got down on my hands and knees, keeping close to the floor, but still everything had to be done by touch. When I reached the area where I thought my helmet should be, I groped blindly around hoping to lay a hand on it, but I came up empty. It doesn't take long before you feel like an invisible force is suffocating you—the same thing that happened to Rich would happen to me. I headed out for a new air tank.

Outside on the front lawn, I saw Rich sitting by himself, obviously still affected by the smoke. Evidently, no one realized what condition he was in, so I called over an ambulance crew to administer some oxygen to him. It was hard to understand why it wasn't being done already, but fire scenes are chaotic and sometimes the most basic things get overlooked. As the EMTs set up the oxygen for Rich, I asked him if he was okay. "I am now," he answered. We looked at each other and laughed for a second, not the laugh we shared at the station watching comedies, more like the one we shared long ago, when a young man named John almost bled to death while his sisters thought he was only faking. We had dodged another bullet.

A few minutes later, with a new air tank and a borrowed helmet, I would attempt to once more reach the second floor to retrieve my helmet. About halfway up the staircase, flames were clearly visible, the fire was beginning to win the battle—the staircase was now blocked by fire. Outside the building, a ground ladder had been set up to a second-floor window, so I climbed up to take a look around. Two firefighters from another city were working a line, but by this time the fire was everywhere. There was no way to get anywhere near the area where I dropped my poor old helmet, instead I just stayed and helped the two firefighters. They were stubbornly trying to make some headway, but the house was lost. There were even little tongues of fire coming out of the electrical outlets, as well as every other opening in the plaster walls. Thankfully, a few minutes later the air horns sounded the abandon building signal, so we were all ordered out of the building.

The deck guns were now being set up. From this point on, the fire would be fought from the outside. It was frustrating to see all your efforts wasted, but in this business at times it happens. The first arriving companies have the best chance of making a stop and our manpower shortage coupled with an order to search for a non-existent victim had really hampered a good initial attack on the fire. Despite being defeated by the fire, I had to be thankful that neither Rich nor I were seriously hurt. There are a lot of close calls at fires, ours was nothing special. Unlike police work, our enemies aren't aiming at us, thank God, because if they were, we would be taking casualties like troops in heavy combat. (The events that took place at the World Trade Center on 9/11 proved this point with a vengeance.) No, our enemy's aim isn't usually very good at all, which sometimes lets us think we can take chances—like looking for your damn helmet when you just barely made it out of the building a few moments earlier.

After that fire, it was a long time before I saw Rich Fink again, and when I did he let me know how much he appreciated my help that day. It was a nice gesture, but I really didn't do anything special. You never leave a fellow firefighter alone in a burning building, it's a simple rule and it saves lives. I always wanted to work another stretch with Rich, but it never turned out that way. I'll never forget the fun we had with that Rich Fink funny bone, it was good medicine for me.

My helmet was found by Kevin Sherman, a lieutenant from Engine 2, who finished up overhauling the fire scene that day. The old leather helmet wasn't too badly beaten up either, at least we saved something. Actually, the house was not entirely gutted and is now completely rebuilt. It shares a prominent place on a street with several other beautiful Victorians. I'm sure Rich and I will recall, whether it's five, ten or twenty years from now, the time we served together and hopefully, we will share a laugh as we reminisce. The two of us will probably recall that young man who came so close to bleeding to death while his sisters watched impatiently, or maybe we'll remember those harrowing moments when a smoke-filled Victorian gave us both an awful scare, but I doubt if either of us will ever miss that part of the job. On the other hand, I'd love to be back in the Engine 3 television room listening to that infectious Rich Fink laugh, receiving my weekly dose of therapy and laughing until my sides ache while never really knowing why, but not caring either. Somewhere out there is a room full of firefighters laughing until it hurts, and that's a part of the job that everyone misses.

THE PRICE OF A ROOM

UNLESS YOU'VE WORKED AS a firefighter, you probably haven't given much thought to the designs of firehouses. To firefighters, these buildings are part-time residences, not just work places. It might not be home, but it should be a few steps above your average garage or factory. In a full-time fire department, there is someone on duty twenty-four hours a day, seven days a week, three hundred and sixty-five days a year. These people need to eat, sleep and shower, the same as everybody else. Yet, the designs of many firehouses seem alien to those needs. The engineers give great consideration to the apparatus that the station will house, but sometimes consider the needs of firefighters only as an afterthought.

I've seen rooms in fire stations with no windows, others with windows so high you couldn't see out of them unless there was a step ladder handy. In that type of station, your daily existence is spent in a small drab cinder-block enclosure. Rooms that tend to fill up with diesel fumes every time the apparatus is started, which is often. At times, we would leave the doors and windows open in the dead of winter, in an attempt to clear a room of the noxious fumes that would linger after a quick run. We even installed door-closers on every door leading to the apparatus floor. Still the fumes would permeate the rooms and each week we would need to clean the windows and the television screens of the black sooty film.

The most ironic deficiency in the stations was the absence of smoke and fire alarms. Not a single house in the city could be sold without having detectors installed and inspected by the fire department, which in turn had none at its own facilities. It always seemed to me that we were courting a publicity disaster with that omission. What a headline it would make, "Entire Engine Company Lost in Blaze When Firehouse Burns to the Ground."

Firefighters would spend endless hours trying to overcome the shortcomings of a building, but with such poor designs and almost no resources, the most they could hope for was a tolerable living situation at best. So when you walked into a firehouse that actually had charm, you thought to yourself, "Wow! Why can't they all be like this?"

That's exactly how I felt the first time I walked into Melrose Engine 2. It had a day room filled with windows, large bright windows, and in the middle of one of the walls sat a large fieldstone fireplace. Now, I don't know if the fireplace was originally meant for heat, but it definitely added a country cottage feeling to the room. The bedrooms were not the seemingly mandatory barracks style, instead there were individual rooms and each room had its own door and window. In fact, each room had its own screen door as well, which was hard to believe. Out back was a vegetable garden, and beyond that, a grassy embankment, which sloped upwards to a set of railroad tracks. Although the trains made quite a racket as they traveled by, the sound of their rumbling wheels and distant whistles added a little bit of charm as well.

Being a newcomer on the job, all I could do was look at the situation and envy the lucky devils who were stationed there. The new men were always stationed at headquarters, and usually were assigned to the rescue company. It would be a long time before I accrued enough seniority to attempt grabbing a bid at Engine 2. In fact, it was a struggle to even get in some time on a ladder or a pump, never mind an outside station. So for the time being, all I could do was covet those berths and hope in the future I might be working there.

Every week, we would drop off the paychecks to the outside stations along with inspection forms for oil burners, smoke alarms and any other paperwork that the captain chose to send along. It wasn't unusual for one of the members of the Engine 2 company to point out the difference in our situations—as if we hadn't noticed. It's compulsory at the firehouse for senior members to torture junior members whenever possible, so really they were just doing their jobs, I suppose. The truth was our situations really were quite different. We did more than twice as many runs and slept in a barracks-style bedroom with at least five other firefighters at headquarters—a station that had all the atmosphere of a barn with some of the farm animals still roaming around. So the Engine 2 crew gloated at our fate and we pretended we didn't care. They didn't buy it.

Once in a while, there would be a vacancy up at Engine 2, due to vacations or sickness. When the occasion did arise, some senior man would always selflessly volunteer to go. Now you know that it had to be a good deal when a senior man volunteered, because anything that had the slightest drawback was immediately unloaded on a junior man. Each man had been a rookie at one time and they seemed to relish the fact that someone else now occupied that unenviable position. The knowledge of how much a junior man would enjoy working a shift at an outside station only made it that much sweeter for the senior man that went in his place. I must have been on the job close to a year before I would get a chance to spend a single night at Engine 2. If I had thought about it, I probably could have predicted the exact circumstances that would have allowed such a thing to happen.

It was about 6.00 p.m. on the second night of our two night shifts. We worked an eight-day cycle that started with two days on, followed by two nights on and then four days off. A firefighter from Engine 2 had called in sick and they needed a replacement for the night. Normally, a senior man would volunteer to spend the night at Engine 2 in a heartbeat, but since it was our second night they had already made their beds. This small inconvenience changed everything. Even though it would take but a few minutes to break down a bed and make a new one up at Engine 2, it was an inconvenience, and that's all it took. No, this was out of the question, send a junior man. This was the only list on which I had number one status.

They all had a few laughs as I packed up some things, grabbed my gear and headed for "Two" for the night. "See ya, rookie," echoed off my back as I walked down the corridor to leave. Little did they know how happy I was to be heading out. In fact, if they did know, I think that one of them would have volunteered to go in my place immediately. So I left, giving no outward sign of my satisfaction with the decision. Engine 2 ran a three-man pump, just a couple of miles from headquarters, I was there in no time at all, and smiling all the way.

Our Group 4 crew at Engine 2 was a unique combination of individuals: Lt. Casey was a Navy veteran of World War II; Jackie Daley was an Army veteran of the Korean War; and Bobby Griffin rounded out the group, as a Marine Corps veteran of Vietnam. They were an independent trio and were famous for giving people a hard time, especially junior men. Lt. Casey was about five feet ten inches tall with silver hair and a silver mustache. He usually wore glasses and was never without a cigar either in his hand or in his mouth. Sometimes the cigar was lit and sometimes it wasn't, but it was almost always there. When you talked to Lt. Casey, he would squint his eyes and play with his cigar while he stared at you as if he was considering every word that you said.

John Jeremiah Daley was the private that I would be working with on the pump. Everyone called him Jackie. He was about five feet six inches tall, one hundred and fifty pounds, with blue eyes and hair that was beginning to turn gray. Jack was a human dynamo. I don't think that he ever stood perfectly still. He was always up on the balls of his feet, jingling the change in his pocket, his eyes constantly darting around the room as if he was on edge. He had a reputation as a good guy, but one who didn't take much nonsense from anybody, unless it was done with a smile. Jack's demeanor was always very animated and he usually had a look of mischief in those blue eyes. If you stepped on his toes, he would let you know real quick, no matter how big you were or what rank you held.

Bobby Griffin was the man who had called in sick for the night. Griff was a big guy, he was over six feet tall and maybe two hundred and twenty-five pounds with lanky brown hair and blue eyes. It was said that Griff could drink as much beer, if not more, than any man on the department—and that in itself was saying something. When Bobby called in sick for a night shift, there was always idle speculation that perhaps he finished early with his side job and had got into the sauce. There would always be alleged sightings of his truck outside some fraternal organization shortly before the shift started. Some bomb tosser on the group would suggest that Griff was really calling in sick from the phone booth at a bar in one of his favorite haunts. If the rumors bothered Griff, it never showed. In fact, on the contrary, he seemed to enjoy it. His response was, "I called in sick, I didn't say that I was dead!" Griff would be a hard fox for anyone to catch. The rumormongers were wasting their time.

So here I was reporting for duty to Lt. Casey, while Jack paced across the other side of the room. They looked like two cats who were eyeing a mouse. Casey started right in on me, as if they had flipped a coin to see who would go first. "Have you ever worked a pump before?" Casey asked. The smoke from his cigar curled upwards through his mustache.

"Occasionally I ride it downtown, Lieutenant, when I get some time off the rescue."

"This isn't downtown, we do things differently here."

"Well, whatever you want, Lieutenant!"

"Don't call me 'Lieutenant,' nobody calls me 'Lieutenant.' Just call me Casey, or Bobby, or Bobby Casey, but don't call me Lieutenant."

"Okay, Bobby, whatever you say."

"Well, go make up your bed," interjected Jackie. "Don't just stand there, and don't screw up the room because Griff is very particular about his room."

"Which one is his?" I asked.

"Go down the hall and take a right, it's the first room on the left. The one with the shiny floors." Jack nodded his head towards the corridor that led to the bedrooms as he paced across the floor.

I went down the hall to Griff's room, surveying everything I had envied for so long, in quiet jubilation I might add. No barracks tonight, no rescue with 3.00 a.m. runs and the smell of urine and vomit. It was Engine 2 on the back step of a pump and they could harass me all they wanted, it didn't matter.

It wasn't a big room, maybe seven feet wide and ten feet long, but it had it all. Your own window and door, even your own radiator and a shelf above the bed that had a radio and a reading light. It looked like heaven, in seventy square feet, to this firefighter. As advertised, it was as neat as a pin with hardwood floors that gleamed. Since Engine 2 did only half as many runs as the rescue, I could expect a nice quiet night, no question about it. This was the best setup I had seen in a fire station. I made up my rack and headed back to the day room where Jack and Casey were watching television.

When you worked with two senior men for the first time, you could expect to be either ignored or abused. In this case, I knew it would be the latter. The whole ritual of harassing junior members might seem crude to an outsider, but in fact, there was almost never any real malice involved. A run through the gauntlet was expected and the prize of a night at Engine 2 seemed well worth the price. As soon as I entered the day room, they got right down to business.

"How the hell long does it take you to make a bed?" Jack asked. "You were in there for fifteen minutes."

"Well, Jack, I was looking around and checking things out, if you don't mind."

"Like what, going through Griff's drawers?" Jack shot back.

"Oh geez," piped in Casey. "Don't go through Griff's drawers, he'll get mad, he's funny like that."

I could see from the conversation it wasn't going to be a boring night. To let them know I knew how the game was played, I asked, "Do you mean the drawers in the bureau or the drawers on Griff himself?"

Casey said, "Oh no, I would never imply that. You're not like that, are you?"

"I'm married and I have children, Bob," I said confidently.

"That doesn't mean anything today," Daley said with a smirk. "In fact, I don't think Griff would appreciate you going through either set of drawers."

Casey had to stoke the fire. "Although, I don't know, Jack, they both were in the Marine Corps."

Daley had almost forgot about that little gem and he couldn't have been happier when Casey reminded him. "Oh ya, that's right, you're both jarheads," Daley said with obvious glee. "Well, that explains everything."

"You don't like the Marines, Jack?" I asked defensively.

"For cripes' sake," said Jack, "if they're such great infantrymen, why did the Army have to drop everything to rescue them at the Chosin Reservoir in Korea? The Chinese would have wiped them off the planet if we didn't bail their asses out."

"That's not the way I heard it, Jack. They taught us that it was one of the greatest retreats in history."

"Yeah, well, what do you think they were going to tell you? That they were getting their asses kicked and the Army had to save them?" Jack looked at me with an ironic grin.

This is how conversation proceeded, tit for tat, they probed my armor for weak spots and I defended myself as best I could. Daley found fault in everything I did and that included the past, as well as the present. His favorite term of derision was "You're a dink."

I was a dink for joining the Marine Corps instead of the Army. Most of the firefighters who worked on the rescue were dinks. And all of the officers were dinks. At the last statement, Casey stopped reading his newspaper and looked at Jack for a moment and with a wounded look said, "What about me, Jack? I'm an officer."

Jack turned to Casey and said in an apologetic tone, "Oh not you, Bobby, you're not a dink." Then turning to me he rolled his eyes.

I had to ask, "Jack, would you mind telling me why all officers are dinks?"

"You want to know why? I'll tell you why. Because in Korea there were more GIs killed by incompetent officers than by the damn enemy, that's why!" The word was that Jack had seen a lot of action in Korea and by the look I could see this was a sore spot so I decided to say no more about it. The current battle was enough, there was no need to go to war.

It was only the end of the first round, but I already would have liked a trip to the pharmacy for some antacids. Jack scrutinized every move I made and analyzed every word I said. He was like a district attorney prosecuting a case. Casey pretended to be an innocent bystander but was real quick to point out anything that Jack may have overlooked. Our shift began at 6.00 p.m. By 8.00 p.m., I had been called a dink countless times. I was already a dinkish dink, a dinkinarian, and the duke of dinkdom. It was beautiful lodgings alright, but I was going to pay for my room and board in a big way.

Luckily, that night there was a hockey game on the tube. Jack happened to be a huge hockey fan, so for a while his attention was diverted away from me as the game got underway. Well, at least for a little while. Soon Jack was out of his seat pacing around the room supplying Casey and myself with a running commentary. As it turned out, I was in good company because most of the hockey players were being described as dinks, too. In fact, the coach on one of the teams must have been a rather large fellow because Jack said he was the biggest dink of all.

While Jack concentrated on his new targets, I turned my attention to the daily newspaper. During the work week, I never seemed able to find time to read the daily news, so when I worked nights I looked forward to perusing all the papers left behind by the day shift. Unfortunately, Jack began asking me questions about the ongoing hockey game and since this dink wasn't watching it, I didn't have any answers. As an avid hockey fan, he couldn't understand how my attention could be diverted from the television, which was situated directly in front of me, even though it was obvious to everyone that I was reading the paper. It didn't matter that Casey was lost in some magazine on the other side of the room. No, he had given up on Casey a long time ago. Since I was replacing Griffin, who was a huge hockey fan, then it was mandatory that I be interested in the game—at least according to Jack's logic.

Determined to read the newspaper, I ignored all of Jack's badgering. Finally, in exasperation, he grabbed the end of the recliner in which I was sitting and turned it so it faced the wall instead of the television. "Now you can read your newspaper without the TV distracting you!"

I took a long look at him. "You really are a bit of a psycho, aren't you, Jack?"

"No, I'm not a psycho," said Jack "It's just unusual to have someone here who doesn't like sports. Most of the guys at Two like sports, you know what I mean?"

"I like sports, Jack!"

"Oh yeah, well what sports do you like?"

"I like football, I like boxing ..."

"Boxing," he interjected, "that's not a sport!"

"Boxing is not a sport, Jack? Why isn't boxing a sport?"

"You dink, haven't you ever noticed in a real sport there is usually a bat, a ball or a puck or something? You don't just show up and start slugging each other like two goons! Plus, they're all a bunch of babies anyway."

I knew I should resist the temptation to be involved in this insane debate, but somehow I couldn't stop myself.

"So professional fighters are babies, how did you come up with that, Jack?"

"Well that's simple. Maybe if you had been watching the hockey game, you would have noticed that when hockey players fight they take off their gloves because they mean business. When boxers fight they put their big cushy gloves on because they don't want to get hurt—they're a bunch of babies."

"Jack, I can tell you when you get hit with those gloves by someone who knows how to throw a punch it does a considerable amount of damage."

"Well, they could do a lot more damage if they didn't have the gloves on," Jack replied. "And how would you know anyway have you ever been hit by one?"

"Well, as a matter of fact I have, Jack."

At this statement, Casey turned his head toward me, peering out of his squinting eyes and all the while playing with his unlit cigar. After a few seconds of looking at me, he said, "What made you take up boxing, do you like hitting people?" I could see from the look on Jack's face he welcomed Casey joining in on the harassment.

"No, it's not that I enjoy hitting people, Bobby. It was just for the fun of it, down at a local gym. You know, get some exercise while getting some aggression out at the same time."

"Why do you have a lot of pent up aggression inside of you?" Casey asked looking at me quizzically. He removed the cigar from his mouth and said, "Did anyone ever tell you that one of the most serious offenses you can commit on this job is striking an officer?"

"What do you think he's going to do, punch you out, Casey?" Jack said, as he laughed out loud.

"No, I don't think he'd ever punch me or anything," Casey replied. Then he quickly shot me a glance and said, "You wouldn't, would you? You don't have any of these pent-up frustrations against me, do you? I mean, we don't even know each other that well!"

Casey's tone of voice and demeanor seemed to suggest there might be a homicidal maniac in the room. Jack laughed at Casey's supposed trepidation and told him to calm down. "I'm calm," said Casey. "I just think that it's important that someone new on the job understands how serious an offense striking an officer is!"

About this time, I should have walked over to the double hung window, raised the bottom sash, placed my hand on the sill and slammed it down on my fingers. Then I could have turned to the both of them and said, "It's been really nice talking to the two of you, good night!" But if I did that they would have won, because this was really just a game. My only hope was to try to steer the conversation in a new direction—at least it was worth a try.

"By the way," I said. "I've been coming up here bringing you your paychecks and paperwork for almost a year, and all the time looking at this beautiful stone fireplace that never once have I seen so much as an ash inside the grate. Doesn't anyone ever use it?" Jack took the bait immediately.

"Ya, we use it sometimes."

"Sometimes? Like when, Jack?" I replied.

"Why, would you like a fire? Is that what you're looking for?"

"Sure, that would be great, Jack, if you're serious, but you probably don't even have any wood."

"Don't worry about us. We have plenty of wood, get up off your arse and come with me, kid."

This new tactic worked beautifully. Now Jack was on the defensive. So down we went into the basement, and sure enough there must have been a cord of wood stacked neatly against the wall. You could have put a level on the top of it, the wood was stacked so evenly. I almost hated to disturb the precision of its lines. Jack loaded me up with what appeared to be way too much wood, but I had asked for the fire and now he was going to make a point.

Casey looked up as we entered the room and I placed an armload of wood, which I could barely see over, in front of the fireplace. "Do you think ya brought up enough wood, Jack?" he asked with a grin.

Jack wasted no time as he began arranging enough logs to have a substantial bonfire on the grate of the fireplace. Then he grabbed a bunch of old newspapers and crumpled up each one, stuffing it all under the load of wood. The fireplace was bigger than one that you might find in an ordinary house, and now it was filled as if we were trying to heat the whole station. Jack lit a match and the newspaper went up in flames. It had all the appearances of a roaring fire, but as soon as the newspaper was consumed the fire went out. "Geez, Jack," I commented. "I hope you're better at putting them out than you are at starting them."

"Don't you worry about me, son, you just grab on to my coat-tail if we get anything and I'll take care of you. Besides, I don't get paid for starting them, I get paid for putting them out."

His second attempt was an incendiary success. The fire grew until it actually did begin to roar in the fireplace. The shades on the windows were all up and outside in the dark a light snow had begun falling. As I watched the snow through the window, reflections of the fire danced in the background. There is something comforting about the sight of a fire burning in the hearth on a cold night. I thought to myself, this is exactly the kind of scene I imagined when I had hoped to work a night at Engine 2.

At the start of the second period of the hockey game, Jack decided to make popcorn. "Would you like to have some popcorn, kid, or maybe you're not interested in popcorn either?" First of all, I noticed that since the tide turned my status had been elevated from a "dink" to a "kid," and it was a welcomed promotion.

"I'd love some, Jack, and I think I'll put down the newspaper and watch the hockey game with you for a while."

"Don't do me any favors," he replied.

In a few minutes, Jack was back with three large bowls of popcorn. So there I was, stretched out in the recliner, a bowl of popcorn in my lap, with the noise of the fire crackling in the background, and outside in the night the snow was silently falling. Perhaps I was dreaming, or had died and gone to firefighter's heaven, either way, I thought to myself, it doesn't get any better than this.

After a while, we heard some noises outside the day room in the bay that housed the engine. A moment later, the door to the room swung open and in walked a policeman. It was Steve Hurley, who was new on the job, too. We knew each other from the meetings we attended at city hall for our two new appointments to the respective departments. He was all bundled up trying to stay warm. His ear flaps were down, he was wearing gloves, and the tip of his nose was a bright red. The dark blue of his uniform was sprinkled with freshly fallen snow. He had been assigned to the area on foot patrol at night and from what I gathered, it wasn't uncommon for Steve to stop at Engine 2 to use the facilities or just to take a load off his feet for a few minutes. Jack and Casey had grown accustomed to these nocturnal visits. For a few minutes, he just stood there, stomping his feet trying to get a little circulation back into his frozen toes. After eyeing him for a moment, Casey said, "It's cold out there tonight, isn't it, Steve, why don't you sit down for a while and get the chill out?"

It never crossed my mind as to how my present situation might have appeared to him at that moment. After a long silence, he looked at me for a second and said, "Man, did I take the wrong test." Jack nodded in his direction and turning to me said, "There's one dink you're smarter than, kid." Steve silently nodded his head in agreement.

He told us he could only stay a few minutes because the sergeant on duty was keeping him constantly on the move. They were making the rookie pay his dues. He certainly had my empathy. After staying only a short time, he reluctantly went back out and disappeared into the darkness. I couldn't help but feel a little guilty basking in the glow of a dancing fire with a bowl of popcorn in my lap watching a hockey game.

After the second period of the game, Jack said he was going to call it a night. It was early to bed and early to rise with him—regardless of how exciting the game was, or anything else for that matter. Soon after, Casey took his book and headed off to bed. His only instructions to me were which lights to turn off when I decided to call it a night.

A few minutes after Casey left, I turned off the television. It was as quiet as a church. My only company now was the dying fire and the sight of the snow falling outside in the stillness of the night. I sat there soaking it all in, not knowing when any of this might happen again. It was like some form of opiate that could become addictive after a single experience. It was easy to see why Engine 2 was such a coveted station. This seemed like a completely different job than the one I had been working at the past year. There was no way of knowing when, or even if, this scene would be repeated again, so I just sat there in bliss for a while.

Finally, a little after midnight, I shut off the lights as instructed and headed to bed, leaving the glowing embers to fade away in the dark. Now if only the bells would remain silent to shift change, I thought, as I climbed into bed, that would be a perfect ending. The bed came equipped with a reading light, so I snapped it on and grabbed a few magazines. Before long, I noticed it was awfully cold in the room. There was an extra blanket at the foot of the bed that I added to the mix, and once again began to read. As I lay there reading, suddenly I realized it was so cold I could see my breath. I thought to myself, what the hell is going on in here? Since each room had its own radiator, it was time to check and see if it was working—maybe Griff was a nature lover and liked sleeping in an icebox. A quick inspection revealed the valve on the radiator was open so that wasn't the problem, but the radiator was stone cold. Perhaps the senior men were having a little fun at the rookie's expense was my next thought. So off I went to do a little investigating and to find out if the thermostat, that controlled the heat to the room, had been turned down by some prankster.

Up and down the dimly lit corridor, I searched for a thermostat, but to no avail. It had to be done quietly because the last thing I wanted to do was wake up Jack. With a soft tread I searched the corridors for some sign of a heat control, but none was found. All the while waiting to hear Jack's voice ask sarcastically, "What are you up to, you dink?"

I headed for the day room where we all had sat watching the game earlier and there, mounted on the wall by the door, was a thermostat. Well, hallelujah, I thought to myself, as I went over to check the radiator and see if it was working. It was ice cold just like the bedrooms. The only thing I could think of was it might be malfunctioning, so I turned it up a few degrees and headed back to the bedroom to await the results.

It was too late at night for this nonsense. What I really wanted now was to get a little sleep. In a few minutes, the old pipes began banging and then the hiss of the steam could be heard as the radiators came to life. It was music to my ears, the gray cast iron was singing away as I turned out the lights and shut my tired eyes.

Some time later, I awoke tossing and turning in the bed. What was once a frigid room had now grown uncomfortably warm. I threw off the extra blanket and opened the door to the room. What a wacky heating system, I thought to myself. First it was as cold as ice and now it's hotter than hell. The good news was every room had its own window, so I opened the bottom sash about six inches and climbed back into bed. It definitely seemed a little strange to have heat pouring out of the radiator with the window open right above it, but it was the middle of the night and it was the only adjustment I could think of that would fix the problem. So Engine 2 wasn't perfect after all, but I could live with its shortcomings. In a few minutes, the winter air cooled the room enough so I could settle down and fall to sleep.

The next thing I remember was being awakened by a loud roar that seemed to shake the building to its foundation. What now? I thought. Were we having an earthquake or did the boiler explode from producing all that steam? Then I heard the train whistle, it was just the first commuter train of the day rumbling past the building. I looked at the clock and it read just a few minutes after 5.30 a.m. This definitely wouldn't be my first choice in alarm clocks, I can tell you. I wondered if anyone ever got to the point where they could sleep through such a racket? There was still time to catch a quick nap since my relief wasn't due to almost seven. At 6.00 a.m. sharp, Jack was up closing doors and walking around the corridors. He stuck his head in my door. "Hey, kid, what do you think, this is some sort of hotel or something?" Time to get up I guessed, but still I lay there for another twenty minutes examining the cracks in the ceiling.

After I stripped my bed and got myself squared away, I headed down to the day room to wait for my relief. When I entered the room, Jack and Casey were having an animated conversation that ended abruptly upon my entrance. Casey paused for a minute, his squinty eyes peering at me from behind his glasses. "You didn't touch this thermostat after I went to bed, did you?" he asked.

It was obvious that it was a loaded question, but I couldn't see how to avoid answering it. "Well, Bob, when I got to my room last night it was freezing. I waited for the heat to come up, but after a while, when nothing happened, I came out and just turned it up a bit."

Jack reacted to my answer as if he had hit the lottery. "You dink!" he exclaimed. "When you have a roaring fire in the room where the thermostat is located of course the rest of the building gets cold, or didn't you think of that?"

Well, the truth was, I hadn't thought of it. The fire we had enjoyed the night before had made the room so hot the thermostat couldn't turn on automatically until the temperature dropped below the degree it was set on. If I had just opened a window in that room for a few minutes, the heating system would have worked fine.

"*Oh, thank God!*" Casey said dramatically. "I thought I was coming down with typhoid fever or something last night. I was getting ready to go to the emergency room this morning, until

I looked at the thermostat and realized someone had screwed around with it! You don't touch the thermostat, that's the lieutenant's job. Jack, how long have you been working at Engine 2? About twelve years?"

"Yeah, about that long," Jack said, smiling from ear to ear.

"Have you ever touched the thermostat without my permission in all that time?"

"No, I wouldn't dare," said Daley with the sanctity of a saint.

"You know what you are?" Casey said to me, "You're a dial twister!"

Somehow, he made this sound as if it was one of the most abhorrent behavioral traits known to man. He immediately walked over, picked up the phone that connected Engine 2 to headquarters and said, "Get the captain on the phone," to the dispatcher. Oh, but didn't I wish at that moment that I had never admitted to doing anything. A rookie mistake for sure because, as I would learn, honesty doesn't always pay off at the firehouse—especially in this type of situation.

Daley was up on the balls of his feet now, shaking the change in his pockets with a big smile plastered across his face. "You're in trouble now, kid," he advised. "You screwed up royally, you'll never get back up here again." My first tour spent up at Engine 2 would probably be my last. After a few moments, Casey got the captain on the phone.

"Cap, you know this guy you sent up here last night? Yeah, that's right, the McCourt guy. Well, don't send him up here anymore. Send up someone else next time. Why? I'll tell you why, because he's a dial twister. A dial twister!" He repeated loudly. I could only imagine what the captain was thinking on the other end of the line. "After we went to bed last night he was playing with the thermostat and he had it hotter than an oven in here. I lay in bed half the night drenched in sweat, wondering if I'd make it till the morning. So Cap, next time Griff or Jack are out, send up one of the other guys alright? Okay, Cap, thanks. I'll talk to you later."

It was only a brief conversation, but that was all that was needed. I knew every detail of it was now being told to the rest of the group downtown. When I returned to my own station in four days, I was going to be known as the dial-twisting dink who was expelled from Engine 2. The prospect of that certainly wasn't something I was too happy about, but for the time being I just wanted to exit the premises.

Soon, the first member of the day shift arrived for duty. Before he could even put his gear on the engine, Daley was telling him all about the rookie screw-up. It was Jack's relief who was reporting for duty, but you could tell he hated to leave, he was enjoying my predicament to the point where I could have strangled him. He reluctantly headed towards the door, but couldn't resist a quick barb before leaving. "See you later, *dial twister*," was all I heard through the closing door, as he walked out grinning from ear to ear.

Casey sat there just sipping his coffee. He was alternating between peering at me with squinting eyes and shaking his head in utter disbelief. He was playing it to the hilt. There was nothing in this world more incomprehensible than the idea of a rookie touching a thermostat that he had personally set. When my relief came I wasted no time in gathering up my gear and fleeing the scene of the alleged crime. Quick enough, I might add, to avoid another retelling of my misfortunes to the newly arriving firefighter.

On my four days off, I didn't run into a single member of my shift, so I was hoping to start with a clean slate when I arrived for my first day back at headquarters. Perhaps by keeping a low profile, I could skate through the morning and by afternoon maybe something else would attract their attention. At the most, it must have been about five minutes before someone brought up my banishment from Engine 2, due to dial-twisting. Everyone laughed, but fortunately it didn't last long. It was old news and there was always something new happening anyway. That is until a voice barked out over the loudspeaker, "Doug McCourt, pick up the line to Engine 2." Everyone turned in unison to get a view of the conversation that was about to take place. What now? I thought.

When I picked up the phone Bob Griffin was on the other end of the line. Jack and Casey must have told him how much fun they had torturing me and he was probably feeling so left out that he had to call and take a couple of shots at me, as well.

"Were you really in the Marine Corps, rookie?" he asked.

"Yeah, Bob, I was, why what did I do now?" I said waiting for the punch line.

"Well, if they teach you anything in there, they teach you two things," he continued, "how to pick up your feet when you walk and how to make up a bed, but evidently they were unable to convey any of this to you."

"What are you talking about?" I shot back. "I remade the bed with your sheets before I left that morning."

"Yeah, you made up the bed alright, but it certainly wasn't something you learned in the Marine Corps. It looked more like something my kids might do at home, and another thing, there's scuff marks all over the floor. Don't you pick up your feet when you walk? What did you do, shuffle around the room all night? Now I'll have to get the buffer machine working to remove your scuff marks ... shuffles!"

"Well, it's been nice talking to you, too, Griff," I responded sarcastically, "and I hope you're fully recovered from your sick day last week. Goodbye!" That was the last word on the subject because I hung up before Griff could catch his second wind.

So once more the rest of the group had a good laugh at my expense. In just one night at Engine 2, I had managed to earn the name of "Shuffles, the Dial-Twisting Dink." Though I had to admit, despite all the harassment, it had been a fine lodging for the night—although they made sure I knew the price of a room didn't come cheap. In the years that followed, I spent many shifts filling in at Engine 2, but I never did manage to secure a berth at that station. Instead, I ended up bidding for a job at Engine 3, which was at the other end of the city. Although I grew fond of Engine 3, it never quite had the charm of Engine 2, but then again, there aren't many stations that do. Maybe someday, cities will change the way firehouses are built and consider them as living quarters for people first, instead of garages for fire trucks. If they ever do, I'd submit Engine 2 as the perfect example.

SECOND OPINIONS

LYING BEFORE US ON the ground was a boy who was maybe seven years old. As I looked at him, one thing was certain, he was in a lot of pain. His father stood by his side with a worried look etched upon his face. I'm sure our arrival had seemed like it had taken forever, when your son was stretched out before you in so much distress. We had been dispatched to assist a child injured at a playground and the location was a considerable distance from the station. Although we had made good time in answering the call, it's never fast enough when someone's in agony.

The boy was lying next to your standard playground seesaw that, in its highest position, couldn't have been more than three and a half feet off the ground. Perplexed at what seemed to be such a severe injury at the hands of such a benign piece of apparatus, we asked the father what happened. He told us that his son had done nothing more than fall that short distance to the ground and upon landing he immediately began to writhe in pain.

My partner that day was Dick Crowell and, as far as I was concerned, he was one of the best in the business. Dick was a small compact man with silver hair and very blue eyes. He took the fire department business extremely serious, especially the rescue work. Whatever type of injury the child had suffered, I had complete confidence that Dick would figure out the nature of the problem. He and I had a great working relationship, probably because I had no problem at all with him being in charge. When it came to rescue calls he was the man. He was the Lone Ranger and I was Tonto, his faithful Indian companion. History had taught me that Dick Crowell had a tremendous working knowledge of the medical end of our business, as well as an inexhaustible compassion for the victims we attended. Anything I suggested or any input I offered was always taken into consideration by Dick, although his rescue skills were far superior to mine. There was absolutely no arrogance in the man.

After giving a cursory examination to the boy's right thigh, Dick turned to me and said, "Doug, I think he broke his femur." I couldn't believe it, the femur is one of the strongest bones in the body. It didn't seem possible that a three-and-a-half-foot fall into a sandy pit would be enough to break his femur. When I looked at Dickie, he must have seen the confusion on my face as I asked, "Could he actually have broken his leg with such a short fall?" He said, "I know, Doug, it doesn't seem possible, but sometimes in children you find an abnormality or a weakness in the bones that you wouldn't expect—that's what it looks like to me."

As I obtained the boy's vital signs, Dick opened up our jump kit and retrieved a pair of scissors to cut open his pants in order to get a good visual inspection of the leg. When it was exposed, we could see the obvious bulge in the side of his thigh, which would usually be the result of the muscles contracting after the bone was broken. It definitely looked like a femur break and the level of pain the boy was experiencing only seemed to prove the case. Anybody who has ever suffered from a cramp or charley horse knows the power exerted by the involuntary contraction of the thigh muscles. The addition of a broken bone can make the contraction a destructive, torturous process. The strongest muscles in the body are contracting and by doing this the broken bones begin to move through the soft tissue, the jagged edges damage and sever whatever is in the way. If the moving bone should sever an artery the situation can become a life or death drama in a heartbeat. The victims in cases like this are in tremendous pain. Our job required reversing the process and stabilizing the leg so the victim could be transported to the hospital.

Dick sent me to retrieve the traction splint from the rescue truck while he examined the boy and prepared to apply some manual traction to his leg. The sounds of the youngster's pain were echoing through the playground. His cries had started my heart pounding and my adrenaline pumping, so I ran to retrieve the splint like an Olympic sprinter. Nothing's mundane and no job is done casually when there's a person lying in front of you that needs help that desperately—especially when it's a child. Between the boy's cries and the consternation written across the father's face, this call was going to be like working with a gun to your head—plenty of pressure.

The traction splint that we carried on the rescue was an adjustable, one-size-fits-all, device. To apply it to a child this young would require the shortest possible length that the splint allowed. The whole concept of the traction splint is fairly simple. The leg is laid on the splint, which sits a few inches off the ground attached to a metal frame. Manual traction is then applied to the leg as we attempt to stretch it back out to its normal length. Then a series of straps from the ankle to the upper thigh are attached one by one to secure the leg to the splint. If you're successful and the splint has been applied correctly, then it will keep the muscles from retracting again and stabilize the injured leg for the ride to the emergency room. This might all sound fairly easy but when someone's lying there screaming in pain and telling you not to touch them, it becomes a very tricky proposition.

Dick tried to explain to the boy what we were about to do before we proceeded, but how much of the information was able to penetrate his all-consuming agony was questionable. Every time you apply a traction splint there's at least one moment when your confidence falters and you're afraid perhaps you'll just make things worse. The father seemed to be suffering almost as much as the boy as he stood by helplessly. Without a word, we could feel how desperately he wanted his son's pain to end. Slowly and carefully, Dick began to apply traction to the boy's leg. The youngster eyed the two of us anxiously—two strangers, in his eyes, who were now entrusted with helping him through the most painful moment of his young life.

Within a few moments of applying the traction to the leg, the volume of the boy's cries began to diminish. He was wide-eyed and trying to catch his breath, but at that moment he was afraid to do anything—afraid to breathe too hard, afraid to talk, afraid that the agony that was beginning to wane might come back with a vengeance. It takes a while in a situation like this before the victim is able to accept the fact that the pain might really be gone. When we asked him if he felt better, the boy only nodded his head ever so slightly in response. I knew that Dick and I felt a huge sense of relief. Sure, we had done the same thing before successfully, but each time you still worried that this time it might be different. As the boy's cries lessened our heart rates slowed down and we took a few deep breaths as well. One look at the father's face told me that Dick and I had made a friend for life and the fire department had won another vote for the future.

We used a scoop stretcher to get the boy from the sand pit to the cot in the back of the rescue. It's a handy device when you're trying to move someone with as little movement of the victim as possible, which usually means less discomfort.

I was the driver that day, while Dick stayed in the back attending to the boy. His father followed us to the emergency room in the family car. The idea was to drive quickly to the hospital but not so quickly as to jostle our young patient, who by now was beginning to accept that the worst of the pain might really be over. The boy was too young to have any idea of how this injury would affect him, so Dick assured him that everything would be all right. Giving the kid a wink, he brushed some hair away from the boy's face and said, "Don't worry, son, we're going to take good care of you." He was good on calls like this with kids, usually telling them how brave they were or how grown-up they seemed to be for their age. Always dropping a joke here or there to lessen the tension. Honestly, he was just as good with the elderly. Old or young, it didn't matter. He had a knack for gaining people's confidence, which really helped keep them calm in bad situations. Although I watched the master at work many times, I was never able to duplicate the excellence of his bedside manners, he had a gift.

In no time, we were at the hospital, rolling our cot through the ER entrance with the boy's father holding his son's hand. Things had gone well, it was one of those calls that gave you a sense of satisfaction. On the trip to the hospital, I had given a verbal report over the radio to the ER regarding our patient's condition—it was just a normal part of protocol. The reports were always about basic information: the age and sex of the victim; all their vitals signs; and, sometimes, the suspected nature of the problem to the best of our knowledge. Although we gave a report on every single trip we made to the hospital, almost every time we arrived at the ER one of the staff would ask us for the same information—so often, in fact, that we began to expect it.

We had been directed to one of the emergency room cubicles to wait for a staff member to take charge of our patient and relieve us of the responsibility for our victim. The boy seemed a lot less nervous now and his father seemed to be relieved by the calm in the storm. Dick took down their names and addresses since the city would bill them for their day at the park. It was the same as an ambulance fee, only a little less by industry standards, and with nothing extra added for any supplies used on the call. Usually, an insurance company ended up paying the bill, and if someone didn't pay the charge, the city wasn't too aggressive about making demands for payment.

As I talked to the boy, I couldn't help but smile after witnessing the transformation that had taken place in such a short period of time. He wasn't back to normal yet, but he was getting close. After a while, one of the ER doctors came in to take a look at our young patient. His first order of business was to make us recite all the information that had been previously called in over the radio on the way to the hospital. He was immediately disappointed that we hadn't obtained a blood pressure, although I thought the reasons for this were quite valid. At the scene, the boy had been shaking uncontrollably. Between that and his screams from the pain, it was almost impossible to obtain a blood pressure. We had recorded the rest of his vitals, but this didn't impress the doctor at all, he seemed fixated on the one thing we hadn't done.

Dick tried to tell the doctor why we had not obtained a blood pressure, but he was cut off in the middle of his explanation. The doctor looked at the splint on the little boy and asked tersely, "What's the nature of the injury?" I could see that Dick was flustered, he was very meticulous in the way that he did things.

He told the doctor, "The boy has a fracture of the right femur." The doctor, who had been writing on a clipboard, stopped in mid-sentence and looked Dick in the face and said, "Have you seen the X-ray?" "No, I haven't," Dick responded. Dick took a deep breath then added, "I'm sorry, I meant to say he has a suspected fracture of the right femur," knowing the doctor's tone had been laced with sarcasm. In front of the boy and his father, we were trying to maintain our dignity and a sense of professionalism, so outwardly we both appeared calm. Actually, about now, I really wanted to ask the doctor who the hell he thought he was, but it wasn't the place for it.

The doctor immediately told us to remove the splint from the boy's leg so he could examine it personally. Dick and I looked at each other for a moment and then thinking, well, he is *the doctor,* we began removing the splint without really understanding why. One by one we released the straps that held the boy's leg in place. After the straps were almost entirely removed, the boy began screaming as jagged bones ripped through the soft tissue once again. The father looked at us in bewilderment. The doctor shouted at us, "Put the splint back on and have him taken down to be x-rayed!" And with that he did an about-face and walked out of the room. I could have killed him, but we had more important business at hand as the boy's screams of agony were burning in our ears. As we reapplied the splint, we didn't have time to think about the nitwit who had just walked out on us, ruining all the good work we had done and the trust we had gained from the poor boy.

Luckily, the splint went back on smoothly, probably because we had a practice run such a short time ago. The boy gasped a sigh of relief as the pain diminished. The father wasn't sure what the hell had just taken place. He was perplexed, but he was also thankful to see the lines of pain leave his son's face, the day had been an emotional roller coaster for him. If he knew how truly needless this additional suffering was, I'm sure he would have gone after that doctor with a vengeance. Instead, he thanked us sincerely for our efforts and we could see that it was heartfelt. As we parted company, I told him not to let anyone take that splint off until they were ready to deal with the broken femur. Although I was sure that after the episode we all had just witnessed the father would demand a court order before anyone else would be allowed to tamper with that splint.

On the way back to the station, I thought one of us would blow a head gasket over the doctor's actions at the hospital. Dick was mad, but I was so out of control that after a few minutes he just looked at me and smiled. If Dick had a fault as an EMT, it was second-guessing himself after a call.

"I shouldn't have said that the boy had a fracture, I should have said suspected, and we should have got a blood pressure on the boy."

"That's plain bullshit!" I told him. "The doctor acted outrageously and deserved a good smack in the head. That's the only thing I would have done differently on the call."

"He was a pompous ass," Dick added, as he shook his head remembering the scene.

"Dick, if we're ever in a situation like that again and they question why we didn't get a blood pressure, tell them it was me. Tell them I didn't get it, I want to handle those questions."

"You need to calm down." He said it with a laugh, but I meant every word of it.

After that day, I knew my role with Dick would be something more than Tonto, his faithful Indian companion. Besides being his advocate, I'd try to be his point man when it came to dealing with nitwits or any other type of antagonist. He did good work and everybody at the fire department knew it. There was no need for him to suffer any humiliation at the hands of a hospital staff member who happened to have a superiority complex.

The rescue crew worked in a sort of no-man's land. Around the firehouse, your status was somewhat diminished, especially when you were referred to as a nurse or a doctor—sarcastically, of course, and usually by some senior member. At the hospitals, although most of the staff respected us, some of them thought of us only as firefighters, not medical personnel, and that we were out of our league and over our heads. It really wasn't fair because the rescue crews did some remarkable work and here they were getting treated shabbily on both sides. What happened around the station really never bothered me because I could give it back just as quickly as I got it, but to receive it from the hospital staff really got under my skin. We were all trying hard to do good work and I didn't understand who the hell they thought they were treating us with such disdain.

Sometimes people don't understand that usually out in the street where we operate, the shit *is* hitting the fan. Although all of us have been trained, we're asked to deal with any number of situations that may arise—and, believe me, that includes every color in the spectrum. We don't have RNs at our elbows or X-ray machines down the hall, in fact, we don't have any of the high-tech equipment that is so readily available at the hospital. All we have is a few firefighters and a rescue truck that have to perform in the worst circumstances you can imagine—thunderstorms, hurricanes, explosions, collisions, collapses, you name it. And most of the time, it's amid family members who are screaming all around us as we work. To anyone who feels they possess vastly superior medical knowledge, you're right, you probably do, but our training is measured in hours, not years. We're doing the best we can. If you want, we'll take you to the second or third floor of a burning house sometime and we'll see how long it takes before you need some assistance in moving forward, when all your instincts say back up. Then we could stand around and question your courage, but that wouldn't be fair, would it?

One night, years later, I was working on a pump at Engine 3 on a night shift. My rescue days were ancient history and that was fine with me. Now I was an E3 man, taking turns with a fellow firefighter as a pump operator one week and riding in the jump seat the next week. Yet there were still plenty of times when we responded to emergency calls for medical aids and, as a former rescue man, I was given the distinction of attending the victim, at least until the rescue arrived on the scene. This particular night I was riding in the jump seat. It had been a quiet night, so quiet that we hadn't turned a wheel since we arrived for duty.

This good fortune was about to change as a call came in over the loud speaker for a motor vehicle accident right up the street from us. According to the announcement, one of the vehicles involved was on fire. Since our station was located on a side street most of the accidents in its vicinity were fairly routine. We hopped on the engine to take a ride up and check things out, which really only amounted to a two-block drive.

When we arrived at the scene, we could see something burning in the street, but within seconds a civilian came up to tell us that a police officer on a motorcycle had collided with a car and the officer was severely hurt. As a former rescue man, I was dispatched by Lt. Phil Petrino to get our emergency jump kit and the portable oxygen. He told Roger, who was the pump operator that night, to get a line and start putting some water on the burning vehicle, which was, in fact, the officer's motorcycle. While Roger and I went about doing these things Phil went up to check out the injured officer and see what else might be needed.

Phil returned to meet me before I could reach the officer and I could see something was up by the look in his eyes. He said,

"Doug, I don't think there's anything you can do. I'm going to check and make sure the rescue is responding. He's hurt bad." It was unusual for Phil to be alarmed about a medical emergency, but since he had never spent much time working on the rescue I figured that I'd take the jump kit and the oxygen over there and see what I could do. The two and a half years that I worked on the rescue would hardly qualify me as an expert but I had seen my share of emergencies and participated in some crazy calls, so I felt fairly confident in my ability to help a victim in this type of situation.

It was dark out and a crowd had gathered around the officer so I was right on top of him before I actually laid eyes on him. In fact, I heard his pain-filled cries first. I began to have the feeling that Phil's anxieties weren't unfounded. Even though I was warned that it was a bad situation, even though I had heard the screams as I approached, it was still a shock to see what confronted me. The officer was in a terrible state. Witnesses told us that he had been involved in a head-on collision with a vehicle traveling in the opposite direction. The impact of the crash had sent him airborne at the same rate of speed, and, like most motorcycle accidents, it was what happened next that was the real problem.

If a person is lucky enough to just slide along the asphalt, then they might only receive bumps, bruises and some friction burns, but when a body hits something at that rate of speed, it's bad news. In this case, the officer had hit a tree or a hydrant and the impact had caught him on the upper part of his thigh, up near the groin. Just the sight of him laying on the ground was over-whelming. One of his legs was rotated up underneath his back so that his ankle was behind his head and his foot was right next to his ear. One of his testicles had been torn from his scrotum and was lying on the ground in front of him. It was still connected to his body by the spermatic cord, which, to a civilian, looked like a thin piece of spaghetti. He looked like a rag doll that someone had tossed on the ground and had come to rest in a grotesque position. For a moment, I just stood there frozen by the sight of his injuries.

Almost unconsciously, I placed the jump kit and portable oxygen on the ground, as if no longer needed. I was stunned. I wouldn't have known where to begin and was certainly hoping nobody asked me what I planned to do. Under normal circumstances, I would have recognized the officer, but his face was so distorted in pain that I never made the connection. As I stood there wondering what to do next, I heard the sound of the rescue truck's siren approaching the scene. Thank God, I thought to myself. It was like the cavalry arriving just in the nick of time. Phil and I turned as the rescue arrived, waiting to see who was manning it this particular night and hoping that there was some experience hidden in its darkened windows.

We couldn't have been happier when the door opened and Dick Crowell emerged from the vehicle. Happy for ourselves, not for Dick, because we knew what awaited him was a nightmare.

Bobby Kendall was his partner on the rescue that night. He was a junior man, but a good man and unflappable—although this would definitely be a test as to how unflappable. Just as Phil had come to warn me of the situation that I was about to encounter, I found myself doing the same thing for my old partner. Hopefully to try to prepare him for what surely would not be a routine call. In Dick's more than ten years on the rescue, he had seen more than a few horrible injuries so all he did upon receiving the news was shake his head with resolve and say, "Well, let's go take a look."

The crowd seemed to part as he made his way over and kneeled down next to the officer. After taking a quick survey of the situation, he asked for a pair of scissors to cut away the officer's trousers for a better look of the damaged leg. The sight of it was unbelievable, the leg was folded right up underneath the back of the man with the foot rotated entirely in the wrong direction. If Dick was shaken by the sight of the victim, it didn't show a bit. I could see the wheels turning in his head as he examined the situation. Bobby, Phil and I stood by, as willing assistants, waiting for Dick to decide on a course of action. There was a crowd of people gathered by now at the scene but, in a sense, he was alone at that moment, as everyone waited.

The crash of the vehicles, the burning motorcycle, along with the screams of the victim had indeed drawn a crowd, and in the center were four firefighters and a badly injured police officer. The tension at the scene mounted by the minute. A voice from the crowd spoke up. "You better get him to the hospital he needs an IV. He needs to be at the emergency room as soon as possible." None of us responded to the voice, although we all had heard it, we just looked at Dick and waited for instructions. In a few seconds, Dick looked up and said the leg had to be straightened, then he sent one of us to get the traction splint. It was obvious that we couldn't move our victim with his leg behind his neck but as to straightening it, I shuddered at the thought of it.

Dick began to get down to business as I had seen him do so many times before, he looked at me and said, "While they're setting up the splint, we're going to take care of the testicle. Get me some sterile water, a packet of gauze, some latex gloves and let's see what we can do."

Once again that same voice from the crowd spoke up. "You have to move this man, the sooner the better. He needs an IV and he needs to be in the emergency room with a physician."

I saw Dick's jaw tighten, but he said nothing and none of the rest of us said anything either. It was a woman's voice and perhaps she was upset by the horror of the scene, but all she was doing was stating the obvious and adding more tension to the already electrified air.

Once Dick donned the gloves, he made the first part of the rescue effort look so simple. He gently picked up the testicle and irrigated it thoroughly with sterile water, then he placed it in the sterile gauze that Bobby was holding. After everything was cleaned and wrapped, he placed the gauze bundle on the police-man's lower abdomen. An onlooker would have thought he had done it a hundred times before.

By now, the traction splint was ready and in a moment we would begin the unbelievable process of straightening the incredibly angulated leg. There was a huge bulge in the side of the officer's upper thigh where the muscles had contracted around the broken femur. The soft tissue damage caused by the movement of the broken bones was most likely the cause of the immense pain the officer was experiencing.

Again the woman's voice called out, from the crowd, urging us to transport the officer to the hospital, but this time she identi-fied herself as a registered nurse. She was obviously shaken by the sight of the police officer and knew that it was possibly a life-and-death situation. Her constant prodding was doing nothing but adding pressure to the scene. Needless to say, it was causing a distraction while all of us were trying to concentrate on how to treat our patient. It was especially frustrating for Dick. Finally, as a result of this frustration, Dick turned to face the woman in the crowd and said, "Ma'am, I'm only an EMT, you're a registered nurse, you have a great deal more medical experience than anyone here, would you care to take control of the patient and *I'll* assist *you*? We could use your expertise."

If ever an arrow found its mark, that one certainly did, the woman looked as if she had seen a ghost. I don't think it ever dawned on her, hidden in the safety of the crowd, that she might be called upon to step forward and help. Immediately, she began shaking her head in refusal and then added softly, "No, you're doing a good job." And then she melted back into the crowd. The offer was genuine, it wasn't meant to be sarcastic. Dick had a wealth of experience in emergency medicine but he would have relinquished control of the call to a more qualified person in a second, but that wasn't about to happen.

Dick turned his attention back to the officer and positioned his three assistants around the splint. Wide-eyed and gasping in pain, the officer watched us. I'm sure his greatest fear was we might make matters worse. Two of us slowly tipped the officer to one side so that Dick could grab hold of the injured leg to begin straightening it out. It was done slowly and methodically, trying to visualize how the leg managed to end up in this unnatural position and then reversing it exactly, with extreme care. Dick told the officer to hang in there, and that he should start to feel less pain in a moment. Whether he could process that information in his condition was hard to tell, he just stared at us with wild eyes and agony written on his face. Dick carefully manipulated the leg back to its normal position and then began to apply some traction to it. As he did, the officer's cries of pain began to subside. He lay there trying to catch his breath as the traction splint was applied. As soon as the splint was secure, we used our scoop stretcher to move him to the cot and then to the rescue—most of the intense pain seemed to be gone.

The whole time we were working on the officer, our pump operator had been hosing down the motorcycle. He had put enough water on it to extinguish a small house fire, but considering the alternative of joining us in the pressure cooker, he decided it would be best to drown the remains of the bike instead. When the rescue left for the hospital, we remained to clean up the scene, and the gathering of people quietly faded into the dark. After returning to the station, Phil and I spent a long time talking about the events that took place, as we leaned against the engine looking out into the night.

In sixty seconds, we had gone from idling about the station to being involved in what turned out to be a life-altering experience for one of our fellow city workers. No matter how long you're on the job, certain calls still take a toll on you, and this had been one of them. The officer never would return to the job—that was his last day. His leg was broken too severely to ever be repaired well enough to stand up to the physical requirements of the police force. Years later, his sons would become members of the Melrose Fire Department, which seems ironic as I look back on that day. When I was introduced to one of them, I saw a look of recognition when he heard my name. He obviously knew who was on the scene that night, and it definitely seemed to mean something to him.

It had been a gut wrenching experience, but Dick Crowell lived up to his reputation as an exceptional EMT, and he very well may have saved the officer's life. The nurse at the scene hadn't meant any harm, she was only caught up in the drama of the moment. It wasn't the first time and it wouldn't be the last time that someone with superior knowledge would second-guess us on a call. There were times when doctors did the exact same thing. Doctors who, with all the esteem of that title, urged us to take a particular course of action but when asked to help, quickly declined. It's times like that when firefighters realize how much they need each other, because, with the whole world watching, they must deal with these unrehearsed situations and most of the time without the valued help of a second opinion.

STAR OF THE DAY

I

F YOU MAKE A mistake at the firehouse, it is never overlooked. Never! No matter how large or small, it's pounced
upon and, in no time, it's doubled in size. The news travels
through the rest of the department as if it was a headline in the
local newspaper. All a person can hope for is that someone else
will make another mistake, so that yours can be forgotten. But
until then, you are the "Star of the Day."

Eventually, we all seem to get a turn in that starring role. And
when it happens, you just grin and bear it, as you wait for the
next *Star* to make a blunder. A few of these *Stars* seem to be born
headliners, but for the rest of us the unwanted attention is usually just the result of a simple mistake.

It was a hot summer's day and I was the driver of Engine 3 on
the east side of town. The back-step man was out sick, so they
were sending a replacement from headquarters to fill in for the
day. Two privates and a lieutenant made up the crew of Engine
3, and when one of the privates was out sick the other one would
automatically become the driver for the day. The air was filled
with the fragrance of summer that morning, as we waited for our

guest to arrive. It would be a beautiful day for sitting in front of the firehouse, soaking up the rays and solving the world's problems.

Bobby Farr was the firefighter who was sent up to cover for the shift. He was a relatively new man on the job and had a father and brother in our local union. When he arrived for duty, Bob informed me that he hadn't had many opportunities to drive the apparatus at headquarters, so he asked if perhaps he could drive the pump for the day. After some mandatory bitching and moaning, I said okay as long as the lieutenant went along with it, when in fact it really made no difference at all to me. At headquarters, the poor guy seldom had a chance to drive and he really did need some on the job experience behind the wheel. The atmosphere at Engine 3 was more relaxed than headquarters, which made driver training easier on a novice. Besides, it gave me an opportunity to impress a junior man with my vast wealth of knowledge of the pump—or so it may seem to a newcomer, if I could even manage to pull that off.

The pump operator's job never really appealed to me, as a result, I never became the world's greatest pump operator, but I had the basics down fairly well. The job might not be the most exciting, but when you fail to perform that job it's definitely the most embarrassing. What could be worse than failing to produce water when your whole job revolves around putting out fires? There aren't many situations where more eyes are anxiously staring at you than when a fire is roaring and everyone's waiting for water that isn't forthcoming. You may as well be standing naked before the world.

So Bob got his wish to be the chauffeur for the day and he seemed genuinely pleased about it. Now all we needed was a couple of routine calls, so he could get the feel of the job without being tested too much. Within a short period of time, we began smelling the distinct odor of a brush fire. This was an event I hadn't foreseen when I relinquished my rights to the driver's seat. Under these circumstances, it was traditional to start praying that whatever was burning wasn't in our district. Brush fires can be endless hours of unrewarding work, but for a neophyte pump operator it would be perfect. If we were destined to fight some brush now was the time—although I found it hard to even utter those words.

At a brush fire, you want to be the pump operator because most of the time all you do is watch gauges and occasionally refill the tank. Since a house isn't burning down and nobody's belongings are being incinerated, there really isn't much pressure. The rest of the engine company crew has a much different task: they get the chance to impersonate peons. Lugging hundreds of feet of hose over hill and dale, getting lost in clouds of smoke, tripping over logs and choking on smoke, in general, working like a proverbial dog. I should have told Bobby to kiss my Irish ass when he asked to drive the pump, but it was too late now. Maybe I could take credit for being overly generous to junior men. No, nobody would believe that one. I just had to hope that the smell of brush wasn't coming from my district, but that would only be neutralized by Bobby wishing it was indeed in our district.

Within minutes we heard, "Attention Engine 3, respond to the Mount Hood Golf Course for a brush fire." So much for my wishing, the rookie's karma must have been better than mine. Bobby ran out and jumped in the driver's seat of the pump like a kid with a big toy. I climbed into the jump seat with a fond hope that the smoke we were smelling was a campfire or some citizen burning leaves in the gutter. Although there was a good chance my generosity was about to bite me in the ass.

When we reached the golf course, we drove down an access road until we came to a rise off to the side of a fairway. We always tried to navigate the circuitous route, which weaves through the grounds, while attempting to do as little damage as possible. After all, we were driving on a golf course, even if it was a public one. When we finally spotted the brush fire, it was immediately apparent that we wouldn't be heading anywhere else for a while. There was a large area involved on the side of a steep hill and it was going pretty good. I grabbed an end of our three hundred-foot reel of booster hose and told Bob not to hurt himself pulling any of the levers on the pump. He gave me a wry smile and said, "Hey, you could have said no to me this morning."

The booster hose is a heavy rubber hose, like a cross between an ordinary garden hose and the larger type your oil man uses for a home delivery. The pump was equipped with two reels, which held three hundred feet a piece, so after tying them together there was six hundred feet of hose to lug around. I have no idea what six hundred feet of hose filled with water weighs, but I can tell you it's a hell of a lot. Enough to rearrange some of your personal body parts if you aren't careful. The steep terrain only made it an even tougher challenge to drag a long stretch of hose while fighting gravity at the same time.

We chose to climb to the top on one side of the hill and use gravity and the wind to extend the range of our stream of water. This took all of our first reel of hose and half of the second one to boot. Some serious lugging took place to reach this position, but since a brush fire naturally runs uphill, if we stopped it at this point it probably would advance no further. (It runs uphill because heat rises, but if gets windy it runs wherever it damn well pleases.)

In about a half hour, we exhausted our tank of water. The lieutenant told Bobby to break the hose and go refill the tank while we took a rest. There was a hydrant located right on the course so Bob could dress it, fill the five hundred-gallon tank and be back in less than fifteen minutes. The first five hundred gallons had gone a long way so the break in the action wouldn't really set us back too much. Meanwhile, Phil and I could catch our breath and pray for rain.

It wasn't long before we heard the rumble of the engine returning, but instead of coming down the access road as before, he was crossing the fairway, which was the shortest distance between two points. It didn't seem like a bad idea, since the summer had been hot and dry, and the ground was as hard as a rock. But halfway across the fairway, we saw the truck slowly come to a halt. As we watched, the wheels sank completely into the ground until the truck body frame itself was resting on the grass. Through the windshield, we could see Bob, wide eyed and wondering, "What the hell just happened?"

The lieutenant and I headed for the truck to see this optical illusion up close. A maintenance man, who happened to be working nearby, saw the situation and came over to meet us at the pump. He informed us that there was an underground drainage ditch located in the area to accommodate a small stream and evidently our rear wheels had found it. No wonder the pump had sunk. The revelation of the underground stream was news to Phil and I, despite working in the area fighting brush fires for years. Poor Bob was standing there with that "What did I do wrong?" expression on his face. He looked at me and said pleadingly, "You would have done the same thing, wouldn't you, Doug? I mean the ground is bone dry." For a second, I almost agreed with him, but then I caught myself in the nick of time—hey, this is the fire department, we don't give anybody a break.

"No way," I replied, in my most assured voice. "Everyone knows this fairway has a drainage ditch in it." Phil nodded silently in agreement and Bob looked back at the sunken truck with an expression of disgust.

As Bob stood by dejectedly, Phil and I took the time for a closer inspection of the *Titanic*. One side of the truck had sunk right up to the frame of the body, but the other side was only about halfway up the wheel. Since the exhaust was located on the side that hadn't completely sunk, the engine was still running fine. So we thought, what the heck, we'll fight the fire right from here. The lieutenant and I decided to drag another hundred feet of hose off the truck, to make up the extra distance, and tied it into the line we had been using previously. Bobby was told to radio downtown for a tow truck and left in the middle of the fairway to run the pump.

As I glanced back down from the top of the hill, the fairway looked like a miniature golf course with a fire truck as the obstacle. All we needed was a windmill and a dinosaur and we'd be in business. Little did I know what a prophetic thought this actually was, because human nature was about to once again astound me. The golfers that approached the tee didn't seem to hesitate at all. They just put a wet finger to the wind, looked at the lie of the fairway, and at the fire truck lodged in the center as if it were a sand trap or any other obstacle, then began teeing off with absolute abandon.

Soon golf balls were raining down around Bobby, as he stood by monitoring the pump. At first, he was upset and started hollering, but the tee was too far away for anyone to hear him yell, so instead he sought refuge on the sheltered side of the truck hoping to at least protect himself from the club-swinging maniacs. These golfers are a rare breed indeed. Nothing, including a fire engine in the middle of the fairway, was going to slow them down or force them to bypass one of their precious eighteen holes. As I watched from above, I couldn't believe it!

After a few moments, one of the golf balls bounced off the engine with a distinct metallic sound. I mean we're talking about a piece of equipment that cost more than a Rolls Royce and these yahoos were pinging golf balls off it without giving it a second thought. We were amazed. To make matters worse, as they walked past Bobby some of them asked, "Didn't you know about the underground stream?" The first few people he actually answered, then he began just giving them an icy stare. Suddenly, working this brush fire didn't seem so bad, in fact, I was beginning to enjoy it in a twisted sort of way.

Luckily, the second tank of water was enough to knock down the active fire. But we still saved some water for any flare-ups that might occur as we waited for the tow truck to arrive, especially since the engine would definitely not be returning to the hydrant for another fill-up anytime soon. It happened to be a Sunday, so this tow truck would be a long time coming, as well as costing the city more than the normal fee. Somehow, I didn't think it would be appropriate to inform Bobby of any of this at the moment—and perhaps it might even have been dangerous. Phil and I hit a few hot spots while we waited, and Bob tried to stay out of harm's way on the protected side of the engine. The word "fore" now became synonymous with "incoming," but he had to stay there and watch the gauges to make sure the truck was operating normally.

Finally, the tow truck appeared on the scene and Phil and I joined Bob to meet the operator at the pump. The driver had parked a safe distance away and walked over to assess the situation. The first words out of the tow truck driver's mouth upon reaching the scene of the crime were, "Who was driving?" We both pointed to Bob, who by this time could only shake his head in frustration. The tow truck struggled for over an hour trying to free our dinosaur from the tar pit. He tried a dozen different picks and angles, but old Engine 3 was in there pretty deep. Eventually, he came to the conclusion that a second truck would be needed, which meant at least another hour of waiting. I felt compelled to tell Bob that he'd probably shot the whole overtime budget for the next year.

As we stood there talking, a golf ball ricocheted out from under the truck and hit Bobby square in the ankle. He was still hopping around painfully on one foot and producing a creative string of expletives when the golfer came by looking for his ball. At this point, I think Bobby would have strangled him, if he could have stopped hopping long enough. I pointed out the ball to the golfer—strictly as a safety measure—and as he departed I can assure you he was aware that he hadn't made any new friends.

About this time, Captain Zinck arrived on the scene to check out the situation. Bobby, in a last ditch effort to gain a modicum of sympathy, asked, "Cap, wouldn't you have driven across the fairway? The ground everywhere else is as hard as a rock!" In true firefighter fashion, the captain answered, "No way! I remember this stream bed from when I was a kid." I could barely keep a straight face, as I watched poor Bob look to the sky and petition the heavens for an ounce of sympathy. To an outsider, it might seem cruel and unusual, but in the *Cracker Factory* it was standard operating procedure and nothing more.

Some hours later, our night shift reliefs would meet us on the golf course and take over the vigil. With two tow trucks and some maneuvering, the engine was eventually pulled free. The golfers? Well, even with an engine and two tow trucks sitting in front of them they still drove the balls down the fairway with nothing but a par score in mind—that is, until we stationed a firefighter at the tee to put an end to it. It had been a long day hanging around that golf course, but not half as long as Bobby's would be tomorrow, when the guys at headquarters enjoyed it all again at his expense. More than likely, everyone the next day would also say that they would never have driven across that fairway. All Bobby could hope for was someone else to screw up so royally that his day at the golf course would be forgotten—until then, he would be the Star of the Day.

A few years later, yours truly would find himself in a very similar situation. Responding to a brush fire at the same golf course, I chose to drive the pump down what appeared to be a gentle slope while trying to locate the engine as close as possible to the fire. Less "hose lugging" was the wisdom of my thinking. Well, that plan worked fine until the fire was out and it was time to leave. I suppose if we had four-wheel drive in the old pump I would have been able to extricate the vehicle from the bottom of that slope. Since that wasn't the case, a tow truck was needed to remove yet another fire truck from the golf course. They were probably one of the only companies in the business that actually had experience in these types of situations. Luckily, we weren't in the middle of the fairway, so there was no bombardment this time. Even luckier—well, for me anyway—was that Bobby Farr wasn't working that day.

ACCIDENTS HAPPEN

CCIDENTS DO HAPPEN, AND working as a firefighter you get to see more than your share of them. I'm not talking about motor vehicle accidents, which are really a basic part of the job. No, it's the ones that are rarely seen, unless you're in the business of responding to every mishap that occurs. Often, it's just a normal everyday situation where something went awry or a lapse in judgment where some common sense precautions have been ignored. Many are just a single careless moment or an ill-conceived idea, where a shortcut taken to save time has been given preference over safety. The sights and sounds of regret reverberate at the scene, from the time you arrive until the time you leave—and sometimes long afterwards, too.

After seeing some of these incidents, when firefighters are at home they tend to become a little paranoid. It's as though all the crazy things you have seen through the years happen every day or occurred just in the past week. In reality, they don't, but they do happen every once in a while when you're serving a community of several thousand homes, and the impact on you is such that it changes the way you view many simple tasks.

"Don't use a flammable solvent while cleaning the kitchen if you have a gas stove. The vapors may reach that little forgotten pilot light and suddenly you will be ablaze."

"Don't walk backwards while cutting the lawn with a power mower. You may trip and pull the lawn mower on top of your legs accidentally."

"Don't clean the chute of the snow blower with the auger turning."

The list could go on and on. And we've seen every one of them—some, more than once, and firefighting is not the type of job where you're looking for repeat business.

One part of being a firefighter is dealing with all these bizarre accidents and, unfortunately, there are no training manuals for bizarre accidents. Many of these circumstances you couldn't even possibly imagine, never mind train for them. So usually firefighters just put their heads together and hope for the best. My method of dealing with this aspect of the job is simple: I just sincerely hope that another group is working when the really stomach-churning accidents occur. It's the "better them than me" philosophy, which most of my comrades subscribe to as well. Unfortunately, it doesn't work. We all somehow manage to get our share of bad calls, but you can still keep on hoping and take comfort in every one that you miss.

Actually, there is one good thing about these particular kinds of calls: when another firefighter performs the old grizzled veteran routine by revealing the details of an extraordinary call they attended, you can counter-attack with one of your own. If theirs was good, yours was better. If theirs was bad, yours was worse, and so on. Somehow, we always have to top each other's stories—whether the story is good, bad or bizarre, it doesn't seem to matter.

It was in the winter time and I was working on a day shift. A fluffy ten inches of snow had fallen the previous night. It was a good day to stay inside the station—if the citizens would permit us. We were excellent at just staying in the station. Not everybody can do that, but we had it mastered. Between eating breakfast, reading the newspaper, planning lunch and watching a movie, there really isn't any time left to leave the station. So when we were forced to leave we would grin and bear it, and then try to get back in our groove upon returning. In reality, we knew the bad weather meant a lot of calls, as people struggled with snow removal, downed power lines and, in all probability, motor vehicle accidents. So all we could do was keep our fingers crossed and hope for the best.

This particular day I was riding in the jump seat of the pump, which was located outside the heated part of our old Mack truck. It was a comfortable seat, but could make for a cold ride. A quiet day inside would be fine with me, and I was sure that the lieutenant and the pump operator wouldn't mind either. Engine 3 is located across from a large park, which everyone calls "the common." We could view all the winter activities we wanted while still staying warm and dry.

As I sat in the day room reading a newspaper, the door to the main floor swung open. A lieutenant from headquarters with a handful of paperwork walked in and stomped his feet to shake off a coating of snow. He asked me, "Where's Phil?" I knew there was only one reason why he needed to talk to Lt. Petrino. It was because if he told me, a mere private, anything that amounted to more than three words the message would get totally screwed up. I sat there contemplating his question for a few seconds, thinking of a worthy answer. Then I told him, "Phil is in his bedroom, and at this time of day he usually plays with his hand puppets. So make sure you knock and wait a moment before entering." And then I returned my attention to my newspaper. The lieutenant followed my instructions to the letter, and after a few minutes he emerged from the room. I looked up and asked him, "How's the hand puppet situation?" He gave me a knowing wink and said, "It's totally squared away." It was this type of respect for a fellow firefighter's hand puppet time that reminded me that the brotherhood was alive and well.

Of course, there were no hand puppets. Lt. Petrino, a stocky five feet nine inches tall dynamo with thinning hair, was as straight as an arrow and he never seemed to mind my nonsense, which was my good luck.

Phil came out of his room after our guest departed. We walked out on the main floor and leaned against the front of the engine to look out at the frozen wasteland—or perhaps just to keep the engine from rolling away. As we sat there appreciating the warmth of the station, a call came over the PA system: "Attention Engine 3, respond to such and such an address for a dog in a snow blower." We both shot a glance at each other, as if to say we couldn't have heard him correctly. Was that a dog and a snow blower or a dog in a snow blower? But when the day room door opened and the driver asked if he had heard right, it was clear we had all heard the same thing. A dog *in* a snow blower. The three of us looked as if we had just seen a ghost. Our imaginations were drawing terrible pictures and no one was very anxious to see the results that this terse announcement might produce.

The *Pride of the East Side* rumbled out of the station to the sound of our clacking snow chains. As we drove to the call, I kept hoping something had been lost in the translation. Perhaps the person who called in this run had used the wrong term, which wouldn't be unusual in the excitement of an emergency situation.

On a call like this, you travel to the address slightly dazed, hoping things aren't as bad as they sound. As you approach your destination, sometimes the size of the crowd that awaits your arrival tells the whole story.

We pulled up to the scene and were greeted by several anxious people. The words "dog" and "snow blower" were falling from everyone's lips. The white faces and wide eyes told me most definitely that the rumor was true. Near the front stairs of the house, people were kneeling next to a snow blower or, as it might be known from this day forward, the *infernal machine*. It was one of the eight horsepower Walk Masters advertised on television during late-season football games—only no one was smiling on this set. This did not look like my kind of call, but since Firefighter McCourt wasn't invisible, and I had Engine 3 written on the front of my helmet, my guess was I should venture over and see what had happened.

As we approached the snow blower, I shuddered to think what condition this poor dog might be in, but surprisingly, it wasn't too messy at all. This in itself seemed amazing. There he was up inside the machine, spread-eagled against the back section.

The long arcing blades had him pinned tightly against the metal. He was in between the blades and the housing of the snow blower—a distance that narrowed in places to less than an inch. The force of the blades had shaved all the hair and a few layers of skin off the body of the poor thing. The incredulous look on our faces was only outdone by the incredulous look on the dog's face, staring back at us unblinkingly from inside the blower. He was a little white dog with fur like a poodle and two black button eyes that were bulging slightly at that moment. No movement was possible, so he just stared at us and made a little whimpering sound. You couldn't help but feel bad for the poor little guy.

The lieutenant asked what all of us were dying to know: "How did it happen?" A woman with a handkerchief to her face, and teary red eyes said, "Why don't you ask my husband?" Then she shot a glance at a man standing behind us. He was about sixty-five years old and was well bundled up for the cold weather. All that was visible were an extremely white face and a pair of hands that were trembling noticeably. He was more than a little shaken by the whole situation. When asked how it had happened, he spoke to us in a contrite and barely audible tone. As he spoke, I could almost hear him say, "Please get me out of this mess!"

It seemed the dog had been tied by a long leash to the side porch so he could get some fresh air while the old man used the snow blower to clean off the front walkway. Suddenly, out of the corner of his eye, he saw the dog sliding unnaturally through the snow. The movement of the dog seemed to defy the laws of nature. Then he watched in horror as the dog continued sliding along right into the moving parts of the snow blower. It was as if he had witnessed one terrible optical illusion. In a state of shock, he killed the power to the blower immediately. He stood there frozen in disbelief for a few seconds before he realized what had happened. The dog had crossed the pathway to the house, which he was in the process of clearing. The snow had hidden the leash from the sight of the man and as the snow blower passed over the area, it grabbed the leash, reeling the dog in like a fish. His wife listened to the story and stared at him icily as if he had done it on purpose—or at least with reckless abandon. The old man just stood there quietly after his explanation, he looked like someone who needed a good place to hide.

Now it was our turn to perform, and we had to extricate the beloved pet for the old man's sake—as well as for the dog's. He would not be forgiven easily if this didn't end right.

Inspecting the situation, we found the blades couldn't be moved at all. They were too imbedded in the dog's torso and to try to move them would probably be disastrous for the dog. The snow blower would have to be dismantled until the pressure was released, if we were to free the poor pooch without causing more damage. The lieutenant asked me to get the tools off the engine. This assignment I could handle with ease, although I had my doubts about what would happen after I brought them back. Would I get the chance to do my constipated chicken walk, which I usually performed following a successful call? Or would the old man and Engine 3's crew swing from the scaffolds together? I brought back all the tools we had on the pump, which for some reason seemed to change weekly. Luckily, we were well stocked that day.

Now, at putting things together, I have never been considered an engineer, but, with all modesty I must admit, I have a talent for taking things apart—especially when it doesn't matter in which order the parts are removed and with no reconstruction phase to follow the dismantling. Soon, we had most of the snow blower all over the front walkway. In the process, there were definitely parts removed that had no connection to the end result we had in mind. The last piece to come out was the shaft to which the blades were attached that still held the dog pinned against the housing. The little guy remained calm through all of this, with just an occasional whimper to which he was more than entitled. As we finally and gently freed him from the pressure of the blades, he seemed to gasp with a long sigh of relief.

The demeanor of the dog was completely passive as we examined his wounds for the first time. It almost seemed that after our helping him, he now trusted us, but really I think that he was just exhausted from all of the drama, or more accurately, the trauma. His wounds were deep, running obliquely across the stomach where the blades had sliced him. The pooch had been lucky. It appeared that no major arteries had been severed and that no bones had been broken, although I would venture to say he would have needed perhaps a few hundred stitches. Carefully, we irrigated his wounds with sterile water, then wrapped them in sterile gauze to keep them free from any contamination. He ended up looking more like a mummy than a dog, but he was as good as gold the whole time. Then the old woman took him in her arms like a newborn babe. Rocking him back and forth, all the while whispering encouraging words in his ears.

A neighbor volunteered to drive her and the dog to the veterinarian hospital. I went over and patted the old man on the shoulder telling him that the little guy would probably be all right. He looked a little relieved, but I think that he would have preferred a written guarantee of some kind as well. As for the snow blower, we just rounded up all the parts we could find and placed them together in a big pile on his front porch. I personally would have needed several more years of education to put the thing back together. The old man didn't seem to care about the demise of the snow blower one bit. He might still be on the hook, but at least now he had one foot touching the ground.

A few months later, we drove past the house and saw the dog outside: he looked as good as new. I thought of how the old man and woman each had suffered in their own way that day and hoped that now they could put it all in perspective, because accidents do happen. We have been to other snow blower accidents over the years, but that one still holds the status as being the most bizarre. And that's fine with me.

EASY MONEY

WHEN SOMEONE ASKS ME what I do for a living my answer is, "I'm a firefighter." Although, like most firefighters, I work a second job. In my particular case, it's trucking. There is usually a representative from nearly every blue-collar occupation in a good size fire department. We are something like a Noah's ark of the trades. It has often been said that you could build a house from the ground to the roof without ever leaving the fire department for help.

Yet, due to the nature of firefighting, I've come to identify myself only as a firefighter to those who inquire. Between the two jobs and the demands of a family, many firefighters work sixty to eighty hours a week. Now, I'm not bragging or complaining, just stating a fact. So whenever the phone rang and the caller asked if I'd like to work an overtime, I didn't automatically say yes. On the other hand, some of my comrades would accept an overtime, no matter what. Even if it was their birthday or Christmas, it would make no difference. They'd conditioned themselves (or perhaps their wives had) to treat an overtime as if it was a gift from God.

I was always a bit more selective. When the phone rang with the question of overtime, I would quickly run the events of the past few days through my head and think to myself, could I stand another ten- or fourteen-hour shift in the *Cracker Factory*? I love the job, but it can get crazy. It's crazy when you're busy and sometimes it's even crazier when you're not. Now, if there was some way of knowing what I would be doing on an overtime, then I would know the answer to the question immediately. For instance, working a shift that consists of shooting the breeze with the guys and playing some Ping-Pong, with perhaps only a few nuisance runs thrown in, would be a definite yes. It's the threat of some multiple alarm fire or a horrific motor vehicle accident at two in the morning that would make me hesitate before accepting an offer of overtime, especially when I was already committed to a sixty-plus-hour work week. For there will be times on this job when no amount of money would be enough to compensate you for a shift on duty. (Well, almost no amount.)

It was a warm summer's day and the air was heavy and still. My wife and two children were out for the afternoon, leaving the McCourt household unusually tranquil.

I was half asleep when the phone rang shattering the peace and quiet. It was the fire department inquiring as to whether I would accept a night overtime on Engine 1 at headquarters. What I really wanted to do was return to daydreaming in oblivion, but the greedy thought of a night's overtime in my next check coerced me into saying, "Yeah, I'll take it." The night shift would start in just forty-five minutes, so I quickly showered and changed, then wrote my wife, Joan, a note. I knew she wouldn't mind because overtime checks had become one of the true joys in her life. In fact, after receiving such checks, ritualistic dancing was not unusual. After years of marriage and two children, it was perhaps the last remaining aphrodisiac.

To cover a city twenty-four hours a day, seven days a week, it takes four groups of firefighters working rotating shifts. This particular night Group 2 would be working. It had been a while since I worked a shift on Group 2 and I was looking forward to it. They seemed to possess an unusual amount of talent. Talent, in this case, being firehouse vernacular for characters who enjoy performing for anyone that would give them a moment's attention.

After reporting for duty, I found the television room and flopped into a chair, pretending to be in an oblivious stupor and disregarding all questions directed to me. New ears on a group have a way of attracting questions, and since my own group had a house fire a few days earlier, I knew they'd want to know all the details. Unfortunately, it wasn't all just curiosity, it was more like second-guessing everything we had done at the call and then telling me what *should* have been done. After giving a few inappropriate answers, I denied I was even there. Someone said they had seen me on Engine 3 that day. I replied, "No, it must have been someone who looked like me." Eventually, they switched to another subject and I slowly emerged from my self-induced trance and joined in the conversation.

At the firehouse, you never know where a conversation may lead—it really depends on the cast of characters present. A firehouse discussion can be like listening to a think tank that's half full. We often dispatch world problems with great celerity. I really enjoy the process and think world leaders could benefit from the solutions reached in these rudimentary think shops. At times, our mental faculties are taxed so greatly that one of our members will fall asleep at a lull in the discussion. This could lead an impartial observer into believing it's more like a vegetable bin than a think tank, but the answers to every problem are all there.

The night proceeded uneventfully. It was so quiet that after the eleven o'clock news I thought I'd try to earn the city's money while sleeping, which pays the same as staying awake. The thought of earning money while lying in bed always had a strange similarity to the world's oldest profession. About midnight, we were rudely awakened by the vocal alarm speaker, which announced Engine 3 was responding to a six-alarm fire. I took solace in the fact that my seat was on Engine 1 and rolled over hoping only the end of the shift would pry me from the comforts of my bed. A minute later, the vocal alarm spoke again, shattering my wishful thinking. "Cancel that Engine 3, Engine 1 you take that run." It seemed the gods of firefighting were going to make me earn my overtime money, and what the hell was this change in engine response all about?

As I passed the captain's quarters, on the way to the pole, I borrowed a line from *Hamlet* and yelled into him, "Something is rotten in the state of Denmark." As I slid down the pole, the captain yelled back, "See you later, Doug, have fun." Since the Engine 3 lieutenant was also his cousin, I couldn't help but suspect that this overtime lad was the victim of some sort of collusion. Later, I would be told that the reason Engine 3 didn't respond to the call was because it had a "mechanical problem." This explanation seemed much too convenient an excuse to entirely dispel my conspiracy theory.

The Engine 1 crew consisted of Lt. Jim O'Brien, pump operator Ed Collina and firefighter extraordinaire, yours truly, Doug McCourt. I asked Lt. O'Brien if we were going directly to the fire or to cover at a station? He said we would just be covering.

Coverage is when you operate out of a fire station in another city, responding to calls received, while their own apparatus is tied up. No sooner had I enjoyed hearing that welcome news than over the radio we were told to respond to a second fire, which had broken out on the other side of the same city. The dispatcher told us they had already struck a fifth alarm on it since most of their resources were tied up at the first fire.

All the humor passed from me with this radio transmission. It seemed like a long series of disconnected events, which began with accepting the overtime, were leading me to this fire. It had an ominous feeling about it. Firefighting lore is filled with tragic ironic twists, and now all I could do was hope this wasn't one of them. As I stared backwards into the night from the jump seat, I said a silent prayer that the three of us would return from whatever awaited us. Looking across a darkened field, I saw the reflection of our red beacons flashing off the polished headstones in a cemetery. The red lights jumping from stone to stone as we passed down the street. The epitaphs written on their faces were visible for an instant as I tried in vain to read the names. The still summer air had grown quite foggy and the city streets looked like the landscape of a dream, as I sat there mentally preparing myself for what might lie ahead.

Our destination was a blue-collar, ocean-side community that had been experiencing some rough economic times. The street the fire was located on was only a block from the ocean. As we approached, the air grew so foggy that you could hear the waves breaking on the shore yet never catch a single glimpse of the sea. To make the visibility worse, the heavy summer air was keeping the smoke from leaving the vicinity of the fire. It was so bad that, between the smoke and the fog, we actually missed the street. We could only hear the radio speakers shouting through the night, as we peered into darkness trying to catch a glimpse of our destination. Yet, less than a few hundred yards from a major fire, we could see nothing. Finally, on our second try we caught the flash of red lights and used them as a guide to lead us to the scene.

My first impression of the fire was that there wasn't any—at least none showing. The structure was a three-story apartment building with a common entrance that was flanked by east and west wings. The east wing was emanating a fair amount of smoke, while the west wing seemed almost smoke free. The scene was more chaotic than usual. The first multiple-alarm fire had stripped the city of most of their own firefighters and equipment, so now all the apparatus showing up for the second fire were from a variety of surrounding communities, and a coordinated effort had yet to be established.

We quickly donned our air tanks, grabbed an ax and a hand light, and reported to a deputy chief standing out in front of the building. He told us no fire had been found yet and he sent us to the second floor of the east wing to try to locate a source of fire, while searching for possible victims. Jim and I headed to the second floor, while Ed helped a pump from another city hook up to a water supply. Greeting us in the main entrance was a large staircase leading to the second floor that halfway up made a 180-degree turn. As we made that turn, we disappeared into a sea of smoke—from there on, we'd be crawling on all fours.

Now, I would like to take a moment to explain the circumstances confronting us. Normally, when an alarm is activated in this kind of building, the tenants are supposed to exit the building leaving their doors unlocked so firefighters can locate the source of the problem. Unfortunately, in some of the higher crime areas, people can't trust their neighbors even in emergency situations, so they lock their doors as they exit the building, leaving strong, well-made barriers in our way. To understand our problem, the reader must realize that there were more than fifty units in this building and now ninety percent of them were locked—and locked with secure doors, which were meant to keep out intruders. With only about twenty minutes of air in our tanks, we had to be judicious as to how we spent our energy, and even a single forcible entry would spend a considerable amount.

Using a hand light to determine which direction the smoke was coming from, I followed Jim down the darkened corridor. We banged on the doors of every apartment we passed, shouting to anyone who might be possibly trapped inside. It appeared to us that the doors were an effective barrier from the smoke-filled hallways and a simple bang on the door would hopefully bring a response if anyone was still inside. At this point, the smoke was getting so dense that only by hugging the walls and shining our hand light directly on the corridor wall could we even hope to distinguish the outline of a door. Finally, we reached a point where the smoke was so thick we decided to do a forcible entry into an apartment, hoping to possibly locate some fire. By this time, it was obvious that there was no fire to be found in the corridor.

When the ratio is one lieutenant to one firefighter, the equation is simple: he holds the hand light, while you receive the honor of smashing your way through the door. Over the years, I've noticed that hand lights seem to gravitate to officers and axes always find a way into the hands of privates. Jim, being the son of a former chief, understood this tradition thoroughly. Opening the door proved to be as difficult as we thought. As much as I like the pick-ax as a tool, for this job, a sixteen-pound sledgehammer would have been a lot more effective, but after a dozen blows or so, the door opened.

As we entered the apartment, we didn't notice any increase in temperature. In fact, the smoke actually diminished a little bit. Immediately, we thought our time had been wasted in gaining access, but maybe it would be wise to take a look around anyway. Jim and I both searched the apartment and then met back in the spot from which we thought we had originally entered. The problem was, we couldn't locate the opening leading back out into the hallway. The only doors we could see belonged to two closets filled with kitchen paraphernalia. Deciding the smoke had tricked us, we quickly took a second look around the apartment. During the search, the low-air warning bell on my tank began to sound, signaling that it was time to think about exiting the building—only we weren't sure how. The second search produced the same result, no door leading back to the hallway. I could feel my pulse rise, even though I knew that was the last thing I needed with a dwindling air supply. The forcible entry had caused me to use more air than usual, and it was running out fast.

Before my air supply was completely exhausted, I decided to clean out a window with the ax while Jim continued to look for the missing door. This would give us a source of fresh air and a possible exit, in case things really got desperate. As I began smashing the window, I heard someone shout something from below. I hesitated a few seconds in case the glass and debris might be falling on somebody. When I continued, someone yelled again, but I had no choice, so I continued to completely clean out the opening.

Jim shouted to me in frustration, "This is insane! I know there's a damn door here somewhere!"

Looking around at him I replied, "You're right, it's got to be here." I tried to stay calm. Jim's low-air warning began to sound just as I heard him say, "I found it!"

When I looked over he was closing a closet door that completely hid the entrance to the apartment when it was opened. It was a simple oversight but we could have paid for it dearly.

Exiting the apartment on all fours, we crawled back down the hallway, hoping nothing had changed since we'd last been there. It was a long corridor and I was out of air, so Jim took the lead keeping me right with him so I wouldn't be left behind. Near the floor, there was enough air to survive, but not without gagging a little with every breath. Jim's air lasted until we reached the staircase, which was a real blessing since I was having a hard time staying oriented with the smoke burning in my eyes and lungs. On the return trip down the hall, nothing was visible but the veiled outline of the tiled floor. We exited the building coughing and spitting, but with the welcome feeling that now we were breathing more air than smoke. In this business, timing can mean everything.

When we returned to our pump, Ed was waiting for us and helped us change over to fresh tanks. Jim and I both felt we had been close to the fire, so we wanted to get back inside the building as soon as possible. Both of us knew if the fire wasn't located soon, the entire structure might be lost and, perhaps, even something worse. There was still enough adrenaline left in us to get back in there and give it another try.

Back in front of the building, some firefighters were trying to stretch a line up to the second floor, so we pitched in and gave them a hand taking it up the stairs. Jim explained to them that we had just been up on the second floor and we had some idea of the approximate location of the fire. So together we all started down the second-floor hallway in search of the source of this incredible amount of smoke. This time we moved more quickly down the hallway, passing by all the areas we had previously checked.

When we reached the doorway we had entered before, we slowed down, knowing that the fire was somewhere past this point. One of the firefighters in the group told us to hold on because we had reached the end of our hand line. We had a quick meeting in the hallway, even though we could barely see one another. It was decided that their group would return for a few extra lengths of hose, while we continued on to the next apartment to determine whether a forcible entry would be necessary, hoping if we did locate any fire that the line would be lengthened in time and ready to go.

As luck would have it, the next apartment door was unlocked, which would save us time and precious air. The unit must have belonged to one of the few trusting souls in the complex. Upon entering, we noticed a rise in temperature and there was plenty of smoke, but still no visible signs of fire. As I entered one of the bedrooms, I heard the distinctive popping sound that can be heard in a house fire, yet I found no fire inside the room. Then as I began to exit the room, I heard the same noise again. After taking off my glove, I ran my hand along the wall and sure enough, I eventually came to a hot spot. Quickly, I felt the floor beneath me, but it was cooler than the wall. I called Ed and Jim into the room and explained the situation. We had finally found some fire. It was traveling through the walls, perhaps from somewhere below, although we couldn't be sure.

Jim told us to wait at the door of the apartment while he went back and made sure the firefighters stretching the hose line would be able to find us. We didn't want to begin opening up the wall without a line ready to deal with what might be lurking within. By waiting at the door, we could insure the returning firefighters would find us, which was something you couldn't take for granted with such extensive smoke obscuring everything. Inside that building was like being in the forest: if you didn't pay attention, you could easily become lost.

Jim was back in no time with the firefighters and a 1¾-inch hand line—it looked as though we were finally in business. As Ed and I opened up the wall, the flames shot out on cue and with a little more work the flames began to reach upwards toward the ceiling. While I watched the fire curl up the wall I heard someone say, "You got to be kidding!" I turned to see the stream of water falling about a foot from the nozzle's end. We had a line, but no pressure. A firefighter called over his radio for someone to crank up the pressure on the line, but confusion reigned outside the building. No one out there was sure what line we were referring to, because, by this time, there were lines outside leading everywhere.

The firefighters with us hadn't brought the line from their own pump and they couldn't remember to which town it belonged. Someone would have to physically follow the line back to the pump and see if we could get the pressure increased, since our inquiries over the radio were going nowhere. Once again, my low-air warning alarm began to ring, which seemed a little premature, but the muscle used to open up the wall had taken a toll on my tank. Jim told me to head out since there was plenty of help and he would meet me downstairs after he squared away the pressure situation, which had frustrated our efforts. When the warning bell sounds on your tank, there is still enough air left to exit the premises, more than enough time usually, but it should not be ignored.

When I went out into the hallway, I knew if I crawled with the hose between my knees I wouldn't get lost in the smoke on the way out. By now, my back was pretty sore from knocking down doors and opening up walls while trying to locate the fire. To make matters worse, all the crawling around seemed to be aggravating the problem. I decided to try to walk upright while keeping the hose in between my feet, instead of crawling on the floor with it between my knees. No matter what, I didn't want to lose track of the hose, which was my lifeline leading to the outside.

It felt so good to stand erect and stretch my back, even for a moment. For a few seconds, I just enjoyed the relief from the pain, then I took a single step and felt myself falling through space. My face mask bounced off something hard with a tremendous force, as I went literally head over heels. My helmet was ripped from my head. Finally, I came to a sudden stop—upside down in a corner between two walls. Although I was barely lucid, my first vain thought was, "My God, I hope no one saw me do that." The line that I had followed down the hallway was not the same one we had brought in earlier. When our fellow firefighters had gone back to stretch the line, they must have decided to bring it up a closer stairway instead. When I stood in the hallway stretching my aching back, I had no idea that my feet were perched within inches of a stairwell that was completely hidden by the smoke. I had taken a swan dive down an unforgiving marble staircase with a wrought-iron railing. If there had been Olympic judges present, I know I would have received high scores on all the cards (except from the Russian judge, of course.) My face mask, which was still in place and supplying me with precious air, probably prevented the fracture of a few facial bones by absorbing much of the impact when I was falling down the stairs. Slightly dazed, I groped around until I found my helmet. Then I struggled to my feet and walked gingerly out of the building to wait for Jim and Ed. (This was a textbook example of why the fire department wants you to work in pairs.)

A few minutes later, they emerged from the building looking disgusted, so I thought I'd wait until later to share my out-of-body experience with them. They told me there was still no pressure on the line upstairs and the exposed fire was rapidly taking over the room. Ed and I waited as Jim relayed all this information to an officer standing close by. We then returned to our pump to get fresh air tanks. To our surprise, there were none. Usually, we carried at least six spares on the piece, but this time, for some reason, there wasn't the usual amount.

At any major fire, there is usually a cascade system present that allows firefighters to refill their air tanks on the scene. We knew the chief of the department was standing in front of the building, so we went over an asked him where we could refill our tanks. Now, generally, an officer would have already devised a system for shuttling air tanks to firefighters that had exhausted their own. Oftentimes having a crew change the tanks for them, so firefighters can take a much needed break before returning to fight the fire. I've had my share of physical challenges in my life and fighting a working fire requires as much air and energy per minute as anything I've ever done. Even the short time it takes to use a twenty-minute air tank can leave you soaked with sweat and nearly exhausted. After two or three tanks, firefighters become vulnerable to injuries or heat stroke, so fresh horses are generally needed. Thus, I'm sure the reader can understand the condition we were in by this time.

Jim walked up and asked this "symbol of authority," with his white chief's turn-out gear and his shiny metal chevrons, where we could fill our depleted air tanks. Then, with a straight face, he told us, "Check around with the other cities because I remember hearing that one of them has a cascade system on the scene." It was unbelievable. He had just told three exhausted firefighters to walk around this huge fire scene looking for help while a portable radio hung idly around his neck. The three of us were dumbfounded. It wasn't as if he was doing anything. He was just standing there staring at the building. In fact, he didn't even seem to be engaged in what was happening around him. We walked back to our pump disgusted by his total disdain for the effort of the firefighters working this fire. Jim asked, "Did you notice the glazed look in the chief's eyes? Do you think two multiple-alarm fires occurring simultaneously could have short-circuited his wiring?"

"It's an interesting theory, Jim," I replied. "But someone better reset his breaker switch real quick or one apartment building will soon be a parking lot."

After a few minutes filled with colorful adjectives describing the chief's reaction to our request, we decided we had to return to the building anyway. After all, we were firefighters and all around us were people whose belongings were, slowly but surely, being destroyed. What else could we have done? Besides, there was no guarantee that all the tenants were even able to leave the building, so we felt compelled to go back inside—masks or no masks.

We entered on the first floor, the smoke was still not as thick as it had been on the second, so we thought we'd be able to operate without masks for a while. The fire on the second floor had been running through a wall, if we could locate the apartment directly beneath it, perhaps the source of the fire might be found there.

Naturally, the door to the apartment was locked, so once again I began to attempt a forcible entry. After a few blows to the door, Ed stopped me. He began to explain a different technique than the one I was employing. Suddenly, I recalled the words of a legendary firefighter: "If some eager beaver ever tells you how to use your ax, just hand it to him and get out of the way." So that's exactly what I did. "Be my guest, Ed!" I said, as I handed him the ax and headed for a hallway window to catch a breath of fresh air. After about five minutes and about twenty blows with the ax, Ed stopped for a second to catch his wind. After a moment, he looked over at me with a sheepish grin and said, "Why did I open my big mouth!" I just smiled and told him he was doing a great job, as I continued sucking in the fresh air.

When we finally gained access it was to no avail, the apartment was clear. As we exited to try another apartment, a deputy chief stopped us in the hallway and said he was ordering everyone out of the building. We told him it was too soon, that there was still a chance to make a stop. He walked us around the corner and showed us a gaping hole in the floor where the fire had burned through and was climbing up the walls. "Less than ten minutes ago, I passed this very spot," he said, "and nothing was showing."

"Let us get a big hand line in here, Dep, maybe we can make some headway."

He smiled and said, "C'mon, boys, we gotta get out of here. They've lost it and I don't want anyone getting killed." By the resignation in the tone of his voice, I knew he hated to leave as much as we did. Reluctantly, we all walked out the front door together as the air horns began to sound the abandon building signal.

Our eyes and throats were burning, the last trip in with no masks had really done a job on us. My heart went out to the deputy, as he walked over to talk with the chief. He had most likely been defeated by a lack of leadership from the man to whom he must now report. As I looked at the chief, I couldn't help thinking of a scarecrow standing in a field, as the birds ravaged the crops all around it. A scarecrow could have done no worse. This wasn't his specialty. No, I'm sure his specialty was sitting around coffee shops with all the esteem of his rank, or perhaps behind a desk at fire headquarters with an officious, pompous air. Since then, I've come to realize that the political nature of the chief's position can breed this type of behavior. The citizens who witnessed this debacle probably didn't have a clue as to how ineptly the fire was fought. For the firefighters, it was an exercise in futility. Without some semblance of order at a large fire scene, the efficiency of the firefighters is destroyed. Certain jobs will be left undone, while others have three times the manpower needed. With twenty companies from a dozen cities fighting a fire, you need leadership. Wars are won by soldiers, but generals can surely lose them.

We returned to our engine and after a little break we approached the same deputy chief and asked him what we could do to help. He pointed out a hydrant down the street and told us to feed a deck gun that was being set up to cover the west wing of the building. The deck guns and ladder pipes are capable of putting out hundreds of gallons of water a minute, but are the first sign that you're giving up on the interior of a building. The fire was already beginning to come through the roof on the east wing. Eventually, it would work its way into the west wing, almost gutting the entire structure.

When I had the chance to take a breather, I looked around at the enormous crowd gathered in the streets. Many of them were residents of this building that were forced to leave their homes with nothing but the clothes on their backs. As it turned out, by the following day most of these people would have lost everything they owned. Every child's toy, every family photograph, every heirloom—everything. As a firefighter, I've heard the sobs of people returning to their homes after a fire, and when things turn this terribly wrong, you want to hide the shield on your helmet. Regardless of how hard we may have worked, somehow, you can't help but feel the pang of guilt, even if only by association.

As the fire burned through the roof and lit up the night with an orange glow, I avoided looking any of the residents in the eye.

We were released from the scene at 7.00 a.m. the following morning. The three of us were so exhausted we were numb. Needless to say, the overtime hadn't gone as I had hoped. Back at the station, the day shift was already on duty. We replaced all the spent air tanks with fresh ones and added a few extras as well. Now we could finally get out of our turnout gear, which reeked of smoke. After eating that much smoke, it takes about a week before your lungs feel normal again and as you get older, it takes even longer. It had been an extremely rough night for the three of us and now all anybody wanted was to wash up, change into some clean clothes and go home. Before long, we were all set and headed our separate ways with a firm hope that we'd never work together again in circumstances as chaotic as the previous night. On the drive home, I made a quick stop to buy some beer. Nothing seems to remove the ill effect that a fire has on your throat like a cold beer or a shot of booze. It probably sounds like an excuse to drink first thing in the morning, but it's true. The cashier took a long look at me when I plopped down a case of beer in front of him that early in the day—or maybe the fact that I still reeked of smoke had something to do with it.

After a hot shower, I sat down and began working the medicinal liquid into my system. The kids were in school already, so only Joan and I were home. I told her a few details about the fire and she informed me that I still stunk of smoke, despite all my efforts. The conversation was interrupted by a phone call that turned out to be Jim O'Brien.

"Have you watched the news this morning, Doug?" he asked.

"No, Jim, I haven't. Why what's up?"

"They found a man in his early twenties dead in that second-floor hallway."

We wondered where, since we had spent so much time crawling around in that same area, but it didn't matter because it was too late now. The news only heightened the frustration we both felt.

After Jim and I finished talking, I just sat there staring at the walls for a while. Thinking of those troubled faces illuminated in the night by the orange glow of fire, thinking of a frightened young man slowly dying in a sea of smoke on that second floor and of a scarecrow wearing a white helmet with a radio draped around its neck. There were no answers, just a hard lesson on how firefighters can be defeated by elements other than those possessed by fire. The tragic outcome of the fire left me brooding with thoughts that weren't easy to dispel. No more news about the fire, I thought to myself. I had already beat myself up enough about it. Thankfully, a lack of sleep combined with a dose of my liquid home remedy finally kicked in and my troubled mind slowly drifted off to sleep. As I passed from one realm to another, I had one last conscious thought, if the phone should ring with the question of overtime the answer was a definite, "No!" Let someone else have a chance at the "easy money."

Victim of Politics

IT'S A THURSDAY IN April, about 3.30 p.m. Spring is finally here and already I'm thinking of leisurely days of fishing. Each spring, I make elaborate plans to explore and fish new rivers. Then each winter, I remember how most of last year's plans were just plans and nothing more. Yet, the smell of spring would stir my blood as always and new plans would be made again—probably in vain.

My shift will end at 5.00 p.m., that's if my relief is on time. I'll start complaining promptly at 5.01 p.m. if he's late. It's been said any firefighter worth his salt complains for at least forty-five minutes a day, so I always tried to do my part. I don't know who figured out the numbers to this particular equation, but it's time tested and true. Tonight, I have something special to do so I'm hoping to be relieved early, but this job has a way of throwing you a curveball when it's least expected. This can't just be by chance, because it happens with such frequency.

The rude squelch of the loudspeaker interrupts my daydreaming when the dispatcher announces a house fire has been reported on Rendall Place. We are also informed that more calls are being received for the same address, which usually means that it's the real thing. Every time "We're getting calls on that," is added to the announcement your heart rate jumps up a little. The reaction of firefighters to those five additional words would make Pavlov smile.

Within a minute, we're out the door. Lights flashing and sirens wailing. We are operating a three-man engine company with yours truly riding in the jump seat. I'll be lucky if I can get my gear and air tank squared away before we reach the scene, which is only a few blocks away. Engine 1 is out of service due to a lack of manpower, so the first water to the fire will be ours. This is the critical water if the fire is to be contained. Once a fire really gets involved in a structure, it becomes difficult to do anything but protect the surrounding buildings exposed to the blaze. In firefighter lingo, all you can accomplish is, "saving the foundation," which isn't a great advertisement in our profession.

Upon arriving at the scene, we are met by a small gathering of people. They point to the second floor where only light smoke is emanating. Their presence always adds a little more pressure to your job. They'll be witness to your success or your failure, with questioning eyes that seem to burn holes through your back. As they wait to see their tax dollars at work—or at least be entertained.

There's not much to talk about when you arrive at a fire scene, everyone already knows what to do. Usually, the only conversation is the officer radioing back to the dispatcher to confirm that we have a working fire. At stations, in surrounding cities, firefighters will listen and wait to see if they'll be joining us or whether the first alarm assignment is able to handle the job. Your fellow firefighters will never root harder for you, because if the first assigned response doesn't handle the situation, firefighters from other cities will be called to the scene to join in the *fun*.

Within a few seconds of arriving, I grab a hose line and head for the second floor. The door to the house is opened already so no forcible entry is necessary. Even a locked door can cost precious time when a fire is reaching the critical stage. At the top of the stairs, there's a wall of smoke but not too much heat. The source of the problem is not in the first room I enter—sometimes you get lucky and a quick hit with the line is all that's needed. To go any further on my own would not be good firefighting, so I wait for someone to join me and hope that he won't be long.

In no time, I'm joined by the rescue company, which, on this day, consists of two men, Joe Nunley and Jim Hughes. It has been determined that no one is home at the moment, so their search and rescue duties won't be needed. Instead, they join our engine company to fight the fire.

The rescue company is probably the most versatile on the job. Once the rescue work is done, they fill in anywhere they're needed. Ventilating roofs, lugging hose or sometimes special requests such as killing the power supply to the building. The rescue company really never knows what it'll be doing at a fire, but usually ends up helping the crew that needs the most manpower.

The smoke is thick, too thick to see, but we can hear the sounds of the fire. Glass is breaking, flammables are popping from the heat, suspended items are burning free and falling to the floor. It's that surreal world that exists inside a burning building. A world you don't forget once you've experienced it. A place where the sense you depend on most, sight, is forced to take a backseat for a while. We follow the sounds and feel the heat intensify. This will be all we'll need to locate the fire. Crawling on all fours, the three of us advance with a hose, an ax and a hand light. This is what it's all about. The suspense builds as we wait to catch a glimpse of the treacherous adversary that grows more powerful by the minute.

When a fire reaches this stage, it won't take long to gut the entire house. Once the heat gets to a certain level, the fire grows extremely fast—to a civilian it would seem incomprehensible. Sometimes, it moves too fast to be controlled. It's like a race against the clock as you try to find it before it reaches that stage. God, you hope it doesn't get underneath you or come up behind you, as you move further into the interior of a building. Yet, with three men and a line, you feel confident that it won't matter anyway. You only need some water, a few basic tools and sufficient manpower to tame most fires.

Outside, the second engine arrives. They must dress a hydrant and lay a feeder line to our engine, before they can come in and back us up, so we are on our own until then. Normally, at full manpower, another engine company would be coming in to back us up; that's not the case today. Instead, all the support is coming from other cities, which are much farther away. Again, this means precious time is lost.

Lack of manpower can be a dangerous thing in these situations and few of the citizens outside watching are even aware that we're running short-handed. (And have been for a while, since a moratorium on hiring was incorporated.)

As we turn another corner, I see the fire for the first time. It's climbing up the kitchen walls and curling across the ceiling. We open up the line, but there is too much fire for it to handle. Jim follows our line back out of the house and retrieves a second larger line. Meanwhile, Joe cleans out a window with an ax, while I maintain water on the fire, keeping it at bay. Suddenly, a firefighter streaks across the window Joe has just cleaned out. His fluorescent striped gear was clearly visible for an instant, then he was gone. We realize someone has just fallen off the roof or a ladder, but the smoke is too heavy to see what's going on below.

The rescue company will stay and fight the fire because a private ambulance has already been called to the scene as a back-up for such emergencies. But the thought that one of our comrades has just suffered an injury is a sobering reminder of the serious nature of the job at hand.

A few seconds later, Jim returns with a larger line and we call for the water with our portable radio. Once the water starts to flow, the fire is quickly brought under control, but it takes the three of us to advance the larger line and root out all of the fire. A line that's stretched all the way from the pump to the second floor and charged with water has considerable weight, and moving it around is no easy job. The fire is beaten, but it was only a few minutes from completely destroying the second floor of a well-maintained home. The rescue company has been invaluable in fighting the fire. The house would have been lost if they had not been able to assist our engine company.

As the smoke clears, we get a better look at the inside of the house. Now we begin the long, miserable process of overhauling the fire. Opening up ceilings and walls, searching for hot spots that may still be smoldering. It isn't over until you've chased the fire down and found every hidden hot spot. I've been at fires where firefighters took a break after knocking down the main fire, then stood around patting each other on the back, only to have a neighbor stroll over and point to a second-floor window, where fire was reappearing. This is the ultimate embarrassment. The fire wasn't out, it was only hiding. It's called a rekindle, and no one wants that to happen. Back at the station, the other groups would have a ball with that information. It would be like giving them live ammo and using yourself as the target.

The dust, soot and heat have turned us all into pathetic, filthy, exhausted figures, but we haven't won until the game is over and, like little boys, we like to win. As we sift through the ashes and douse the hot spots, we try to salvage family photos and memorabilia, which may otherwise be destroyed. When you look around, you can't help but think of your own home and all the keepsakes you take for granted. Here, some have been destroyed, but by confining the fire to a small part of the house, many more have been saved. In firefighter lingo, the results of our efforts would be termed "a good stop." A quiet sense of satisfaction pervades as we realize this and justify the risks we may have taken. There is always danger present at every house fire, it's only a question of how much.

Upon exiting the building, we ask about the firefighter we saw streak past the outside of the second-floor window. We are told it was Griff from Engine 2. The captain tells us he fell from a ground ladder and bounced off a fence on the way down.

"How was he feeling, Cap, when they took him to the hospital?"

"Well, he said he was okay, but he was having trouble breathing, so I insisted he go to the hospital and get checked out."

Later, we learned he had cracked several ribs and collapsed a lung. I guess for a Vietnam vet jarhead, that's doing okay—not great, but okay. Griff spends a few days in the intensive care unit before being released from the hospital. (Down at the local Elks Club, business was off considerably in his absence. When the bartender visits at the hospital and tells him to get well, he really means it.)

Now, the process of breaking down the hydrant connection and reloading the hose bed of the engine begins. This isn't hard work, but oftentimes most of your adrenaline has been spent fighting the fire, so it can be tiresome and monotonous. We can't help but discuss the different events that transpired on the call as we work. Captain Zinck tells us he put a second alarm on the fire because of the lack of manpower, but the outside cities couldn't replace our own Engine 1. The distance they need to travel just takes too long when every minute counts.

After helping reload the hose on Engine 3, the rescue company prepares to leave the scene. As I talk to them a somber thought dawns on me. In less than two weeks, they will be gone, victims of the city's budget woes. They have already received their pink slips and will be unemployed. Joe has a wife and two small children at home. Jim was recently married and has also purchased a home in town. It seems ironic that I should be given such a thorough lesson in what the future will be like without them, just before they leave. The normal good feelings after a job well done are muted by our thoughts of the pending layoffs. None of the usual horseplay is present, instead, there are just knowing glances exchanged between stone-faced firefighters.

I wonder if I could have done as good a job with the knowledge that I would soon be discarded. Would the voting public stand for it? I couldn't help but wonder if the voters even knew of all the consultants, advisors and aides who would keep their jobs, which amount to nothing but political patronage, while young men willing to risk their lives to protect them were being laid off instead. That question would never be answered, for the political sleight of hand had the public totally confused.

As I look at the sweat and grime that covers the two of them, I think of the risks they have taken to save some stranger's home and keepsakes. We know they have made a difference—much more than the public would ever realize or the politicians would ever admit. This fire could have been fought from outside the building with almost no risks to the firefighters, but nothing would have been left but a shell. The public, who don't really understand much about firefighting, wouldn't know the difference but we would. As we leave that day, I make a point of telling the rescue company what a great job they did and how much we are going to miss them on future calls.

––––––––––––––––––––––––––––––

A month later, we fought a house fire on the east side of town. It was about two weeks after the layoffs. A propane grill had malfunctioned and was engulfed in flames. Unfortunately, the homeowners kept it right up against their single family home. The feeder hose from the tank had melted, allowing the pressurized propane to flow unimpeded. It fired off like a huge blowtorch, igniting the side of the house right up to the roof line. Firefighters have a history of being injured or killed by propane, so we have a healthy respect for the highly combustible gas. The noise the gas makes escaping while under pressure, coupled with the sight of flames shooting fifteen feet in the air is enough to make your hair stand on end. It was a dangerous situation and the guys responded nicely. Captain Walsh was in charge and, once again, he proved to be a cool customer.

The tank and the house were extinguished quickly and then we were able to reach the shut-off valve on the tank to stop the flow of propane. The fire was never able to extend into the interior of the house, which saved the owners a lot of aggravation.

Outside on the street, the usual amount of curious citizens gathered to see what the commotion was all about. As we drove away, a woman with two small children waved to us. Facing backwards in the jump seat, I gave them my official firefighter wave, as I do to all the kids who wave at us. Then I realized they were the children of one of the laid-off firefighters. Joe Nunley lived right down the street and his son, Joseph, loved to see the fire trucks, so his wife had taken the kids down to see what happened. As I watched them disappear from view a quiet sense of frustration came over me. Their dad should have been working with us that day. It wasn't as if we didn't need him or he wasn't good at his job. No, it was because in a political game of hardball the fire department had drawn the short straw. On that last house fire, we had worked together, he took more risks than most bureaucrats take in a career at their jobs. That wasn't even a consideration in his dismissal.

I suppose as long as the city prints our checks, there will always be politics in the fire department and politicians will sometimes use us as pawns to achieve their own ends. It may sound cynical, but laying-off police and fire can produce a certain psychological effect that's advantageous for the politicians. The public, well, they love us when they need us, but sometimes inside the voting booth, when the curtains are drawn, they take a chance that they'll never have to dial 911.

CHARACTERS

WHEN I WAS A BOY my mother would send me to the firehouse with my father's lunch. To a youngster, that's an important mission. On the days when the weather was right, there would always be some firefighters hanging around the front of the station. As soon as I was spotted, I'd hear someone say, "Hey, Mac, she didn't forget ya!" They would always tease my father about the size of his lunch, or question the late hour of its arrival. Those smiling faces seemed like the salt of the earth to me back then. My father was not one to talk out of school, so little did I realize what a colorful cast it was that greeted me on those childhood days. It didn't take long after becoming a firefighter for my education to begin.

There are always characters on every fire department. The kind that crave attention, good or bad. It doesn't seem to matter as long as they're in the limelight. Just the nicknames heard around the firehouse would lead an unknowing person to wonder. I'm not talking about the run-of-the-mill variety like Chickie or Bigfoot. No, I mean handles like Wildman or the Beast. A name like that isn't bestowed on just anyone. It takes, let's say, someone special to earn that type of handle. In the story I'm about to tell the some-one special's name is "Fred." This nickname may seem normal, but actually it only proves there is an exception to every rule.

The chief had put me on two weeks of day shifts, which allowed me to meet all four groups and do a little training with each of them. This was before the cities started sending everyone to the firefighting academy. Today, they get more training than a Special Forces unit in the military. Back then, it was on-the-job training under the watchful eyes of the shift captains at head-quarters. This was considered a source of recreation to the other firefighters who enjoyed playing with the new recruit's mind as a sort of initiation rite. As I trained with the different shifts, each group was also taking a long look at me at the same time. It had yet to be decided to which group I would be assigned, so naturally I wanted to make a good impression with all of them. At the firehouse, if a new recruit gets a bad rap, it's often hard to lose—whether it's deserved or not. First impressions seem to stick. My plan was to keep a low profile. Fred had a different plan.

The shift had about ten men on it, and of the four groups, they were known as the most rowdy. Group 2 had the youngest captain and the wackiest lieutenant on the department. All three union leaders were members of the group as well, so even the chief would tread a little softer when they were working.

It was a ritual with this group to always have a big meal on one of their two day shifts. In fact, a person wouldn't believe how much discussion went into the planning of this event. The chef, Billy Stretton, held a lofty position and was exempt from some of the regular firehouse duties because of his culinary skills. My low-profile theory told me to have absolutely no opinion on the choices for the day's menu if I was quizzed about my preferences. Although various members tried to elicit some response from me, I remained completely neutral.

As it turned out, it was quite a spread. Obviously, no one would die from malnutrition on this group. I definitely would need to spend a little more time in the gym or run an extra mile if I were to work with this bunch for very long. Usually, a junior man would be sent to the market to do all the shopping, but on this group, the meal was much too important to risk a rookie screwing something up, which was just fine with me. I pitched in around the kitchen as the food was being prepared, trying to blend in and just be one of the guys.

As we sat down to eat, the captain made sure everyone at the table had met me, so he reintroduced all ten members of the group. When he was done, I don't think that I remembered a single name. Just too much information at once, and the extra attention embarrassed me a little. The men tried to make me feel at home by occasionally directing comments to me and asking the usual questions. One fellow asked, "How do you like the job?"

"I like it fine so far," I answered.

Another asked, "Are you married?"

"Yes I am," I replied.

"Any kids?"

"One due in about a month."

"You have a father on the job in Medford, don't you?"

"Ya, he's stationed down at headquarters on Ladder One."

The dinner conversation was uneventful and everything seemed to be going fine. Everyone was cordial and showed a genuine interest in the new recruit, so I tried to relax and enjoy the meal. I was flying under the radar beautifully.

Then a dark-haired fellow with a few days' growth on his chin and a baseball cap on his head said, "Do you mind if I ask you a question, Doug?"

"No, go right ahead," I answered casually looking across the table.

"Did your mother ever catch you playing with yourself in the bathroom?" he asked.

I set my fork down and shook my head in disbelief. Everyone else in the room stopped eating, too, as they waited for the new guy to answer the question. The whole room fell silent in anticipation of my answer.

I had been lulled to sleep by the easy conversation and now this question had caught me totally by surprise. Finally, regaining some composure, I answered, "That's a hell of a question to ask a man as he sits down to dinner!" He apologized and said he was just curious and could I tell him if I ever got caught in the act. I could feel my face turning red from a combination of embarrassment and anger. I drew a deep breath, looked him in the eye and said, "No, as a matter of fact, I don't think so." What else could I possibly reply?

"It was a great place to hide, wasn't it?" he said with a satisfied grin.

Everyone started laughing and I laughed, too, but I think my face was red for at least ten minutes and I don't think I tasted another morsel of food. Needless to say, at the end of the day, there was at least one name I remembered of the ten men who sat down to eat that day—and I think that's all Fred ever wanted.

At the time, I was working the rescue truck and most of our calls were medical aids. So around the station, we were sarcastically referred to as *Doctors* and *Nurses*, because of our medical expertise.

In the barrack style of bedrooms where we slept, there were six beds and more than once I shared a room with Fred. One morning, as we dressed after a night shift, he asked me if I could do him a favor. Forgetting who I was talking to, I said, "Sure." He then explained that he had a boil on his ass and he wanted to know what I thought of it. I told him I didn't really know much about boils and didn't think I could help him with a diagnosis. Yet, he claimed out of camaraderie, I should at least take a look at it. Before I could object, he bent over and pulled his pants down and mooned me. Here was his white hairy arse staring me in the face, while he keenly awaited my assessment of his medical problem. And like a fool, in a moment of hesitation, I found myself staring at Fred in all his glory. When I regained my senses, I told him that in my opinion it was a typical boil, wished him luck and referred him to a senior EMT as I quickly exited the room. In the future, I tried to avoid these insane encounters with Fred, but met with only limited success.

As time went on, I found out almost everyone on the department had experienced a few "situations" with Fred, including the chief. (So I was in good company or we were a sorry lot—depending on how you looked at it.) Fred had been known to use a sick day or two, and the chief suspected that sometimes he might not be genuinely sick. One morning after Fred called in sick, the chief decided to drive out to his house. He wanted to see if Fred was really home or perhaps catch him engaging in some non-sickly activity. Legend has it, he rang Fred's doorbell and waited patiently hoping to surprise Fred, but when the door opened there was Fred surrounded by cartons and absolutely naked except for a beach hat, a cigar and a pair of sandals. As the chief stood there flabbergasted at this unexpected sight, Fred, without any hesitation, asked him if he'd like to "come in and meet the wife and have a cup of coffee." The chief quickly declined and then nearly fell over himself trying to get back to his car. He yelled over his shoulder to Fred as he was leaving, "Take as much time as you need!" He came back to the station all a flutter saying, "You'll never see Fred again, he's finally gone over the edge—he's living out of boxes!" He then disappeared into his office and closed the door behind him. He didn't know Fred was in the process of moving—but that only explained the boxes.

Fred returned a few days later, and when questioned about what happened, he repeated his famous quote, "What happens to most people once in a lifetime, happens to me on a daily basis." This was not an idle boast.

One day, I overheard three captains discussing who would have the privilege of leading Fred. After a few heated exchanges, the senior captain told his junior comrades, "I had him! He had him! And now you got him and you're stuck with him!" Yes, the Fred sweepstakes were brief and to the point: low man gets the *prize*.

Yet, despite the long list of firefighters who would have loved to strangle Fred, he had some supporters as well. No one was more patient with Fred than the union president, J.P. O'Neil. J.P. was famous for defending his men against angry chiefs and city lawyers. Naturally, Fred, with all his crazy antics, gave J.P. more than one chance to exercise his expertise in protecting his union members, but it was a love-hate relationship. As much as Fred riled him by putting him in the hot seat as a union officer, he also entertained him with some of the most comic moments of his career.

At headquarters, there was a gym and sauna up on the top floor. The gym could be used anytime, but the sauna only while off duty, for obvious reasons. Well, one day, J.P. invited a union official from another city to come by and take a sauna while they talked a little union business. The two of them were in there getting a good sweat going when the door popped open and in walked Fred. Now, there would be nothing unusual about this except at the time he was fully clothed and wearing a baseball cap with sunglasses. He proceeded to casually take a seat next to them and asked them how they were doing. J.P. introduced his guest to Fred and then continued to discuss union business. Fred just sat there quietly, as if he didn't have a care in the world. After a few minutes J.P.'s guest looked at him and nodded his head towards Fred as if to say "What the hell is going on with this guy, Jack?" I mean, it's maybe 120 degrees Fahrenheit and Fred had been sitting there fully clothed not saying a word. Finally, sensing his buddy's anxiety, an exasperated J.P. asked Fred, "Aren't you a little uncomfortable being in here fully clothed?"

Fred calmly replied, "No, actually I've been cold all day and this is the first time I've felt normal."

If anybody had wondered what it might take to make Fred normal, well, now we knew: put him in a superheated sauna fully clothed with sunglasses and a baseball cap. Fred had a way of turning the most mundane moments of a tour of duty into memorable events. Sometimes we loved him for it, and other times we wanted to kill him.

Eventually, Fred retired with over thirty years on the job. By then, he had performed enough feats to fill a Russian novel, but there were still some classic moments to come. Every once in a while, he'd drop by Engine 3 to use the facilities. He was taking a shower one day when some insurance salesmen stopped by to educate us about our life insurance options. They love talking to firefighters because we're a captive audience and work in a dangerous occupation. If a firefighter ever prays for an alarm to sound, it's when a salesman has us cornered in the station. In the middle of the agents' spiel, Fred emerged from the bathroom with only a towel wrapped around his waist and a pair of shower thongs on his feet. That might seem harmless to normal people, but the firefighters knew better.

He expressed a great interest in the subject at hand and soon engaged both of the salesmen into explaining the finer points of life insurance and all of its benefits, specifically to him. Naturally, they were more than willing, sensing a possible sale. As they started to explain all the wonderful benefits of life insurance, which they were taking quite seriously, Fred's towel fell to the floor. Fred waited a moment and then calmly picked up the towel and wrapped it around his neck without batting an eyelash, leaving nothing below the towel but his shower thongs. The salesmen continued with the dissertation, but it was obvious that their hearts weren't in it anymore. Their eyes were getting glassy and were abnormally fixed above Fred's waist in their focus. Soon, they were talking about leaving literature and coming back at a later date after everyone had a chance to read the brochures. All the time, Fred stood about two feet from them holding the ends of the towel, which was still wrapped around his neck, and acting as if he was completely mesmerized by every word they said. The firefighters in the room sat watching this scene with hidden grins behind their poker faces, waiting to see how long the salesmen could last. Fred, at one time or another, had done something similar to almost all of us, but this time it was someone else, and the firefighters were enjoying every minute of it.

Many "Fred-less" years lie ahead of me at the firehouse, as I write this story, and I know other characters will come along to entertain us. They always say nothing changes but the names. Yet, I don't think anyone will ever duplicate the status of Fred in the minds of the men who worked with him. And from the first time I met him, I think that's all he ever wanted.

PULLBOXES AND PIANOS

ASK A FIREFIGHTER WHAT he does on a night shift and the answer will always be the same: hopefully, sleep. For if we do manage to get a half-decent night's sleep, it enables us to lead productive lives the following day. Whether it's working a side job or just doing chores around the house, everyone needs a certain amount of sleep. Sleep is like a medicinal balm, which makes every facet of life easier. Without enough of it, a body can spend the next day languishing in a sleep-deprived stupor, unable to escape the effects of the previous night. I'm not saying you shouldn't be allowed to disturb a sleeping firefighter at night—although there are some among us who consider it a criminal act—no, I just think that any reasonable person, given the option, would rather pass the night in the realm of sweet forgetfulness. Unfortunately, it's an area in which we don't get much sympathy from the general public. Most citizens feel, since they're paying our salaries, they couldn't care if our eyelashes ever touch for more than a second when we work a night shift—and I suppose that's human nature, too.

Perhaps if we worked every night, there would be a certain continuity to the process, but since we only work a few nights a week, we're never really able to find a rhythm. So I began each nighttime shift with the fondest wish: that after the midnight hour, the tires of the pump would not rotate until the crew for morning shift arrived. In order to achieve this nocturnal goal, there are a variety of factors that must occur. For instance, all the fire and smoke alarms in the city need to remain silent for the night. That may not sound difficult, but if you counted every one of those sleep interrupters in the entire city, the odds of them all being quiet for the whole night is far from a sure thing. Well, if there are no fires, they won't sound, right? Wrong. "Cause unknown" is a term that describes many of the alarms to which we respond; some other reasons might be burning toast, someone sneaking a cigarette, or a renegade arachnid whose wispy web mimics smoke to a smoke detector. If a spider that has tripped an alarm had the ability to speak, he might say, "What the hell was so special about that stretch of web to start horns blaring and lights flashing?" And we firefighters all blurry-eyed staring at him, cursing his very existence. (As a firefighter, I must state here that the advent of the smoke detector has proven tremendously effective in the prevention of loss of life. No one can dispute that, not even a sleep-deprived firefighter.)

Not every night is equal either. Weekends and holidays are far more active than your ordinary weekday night. It's the ritual celebrations, which occur when there is no work the next day, that end with many a call to the fire department. The midnight hours also lend a little magic to the mix. Sometimes, the red lights pretend they're green, the stop signs hide their faces and the walls and fences disguise themselves as new streets or driveways. Citizens, returning from a night's festivities, are deceived, and the result of these witching hours is twisted metal or worse. So on weekends and holidays, most firefighters stay up a little later, at least until the bulk of the celebrants are home, and then hope that the remaining stragglers can find their way without the need of our assistance.

There is one sleep disturbance that is much more annoying than all the others: when some mischievous hand opens a pull station and drops down that little hook, just for the fun of it. When I got on the job, I had no idea how prevalent this behavior had become—not just among juveniles but adults as well. Personally, I had never pulled, nor attempted to pull, a firebox in my life. Now, I'm sure my father, being a firefighter, had a little something to do with this. But even without this extra incentive, everyone had heard of firefighters being killed in the line of duty while responding to a false alarm. Can you imagine telling that to the old priest in the confessional, in order to cleanse your soul? No, thank you.

The regularity with which these false alarms occurred was irksome, to say the least. We couldn't help but demonize the perpetrators. Why were they constantly trying to harass us? Did they hate firefighters? Was it the same individual every night? Some claimed it was off-duty firefighters coming home from their visits to fraternal organizations. I wouldn't doubt it, a few times that may have been the case, but no one was ever caught in the act—not in our city at least. Now, all this talk about false alarms sets the stage for a Saturday night, as the story begins.

It was Saturday night, the last shift of our two-day and then two-night tours of duty. Friday night had been an abomination with a half of dozen runs before midnight, and then the false alarms kept us running until almost 2.30 a.m. Most of us had spent Saturday in a daze, and now we had hopes that tonight would not be a repeat performance. Since the school year had ended a few weeks ago, there had been a sharp increase in false alarms. The relationship between brush fires, false alarms and school vacation is well known to firefighters. If this was an agricultural entity, the fire department would be spraying in the spring to keep the nitwit population down in the summer. But, alas, no such spray exists for our pestilence.

As usual, we had a few runs leading up to midnight, but then it began to quiet down. The ancient building moaned and creaked at night. The windows rattled at the faintest breeze, but I found it soothing rather than disturbing. One by one, the guys began retiring to their bunks. No one was saying a word about a good night's sleep or a false alarm, without at least a knock on wood. It was almost 1.00 a.m. before I decided that the phantom hook puller may have taken the night off. It was time for the eternal optimist to slip into bed—hoping not to depart from its cotton sheets until shift change.

I never slept well at the firehouse, but I could do a great imitation of a sleeping person. Some of the guys would start snoring as soon as their heads touched the pillow. There was one fellow who could finish a cup of black coffee, go to bed and be out cold in a few minutes. God help me, sometimes I wanted to reach over and strangle him in a jealous rage as he lay there snoring.

At 1.15 a.m., the lights snapped on and the bells started ringing. It was almost the exact same time the first false alarm had been received the previous night. A few scattered curses could be heard about the room, as the men climbed out of their racks. Sliding down the poles to the apparatus, we were all counting the bells in our heads. Someone yelled, "That's Box 19, you know it's a falsie!" Box 19 was in a deserted part of town, and was one of the longest runs from the station. Two engines, a ladder and a rescue sped down the street to answer Box 19. We have to treat them all the same, even when we suspect it's false—no one can ever be sure. At a city hall meeting, an elected official suggested once that we should respond to false alarms with less apparatus. Oh, I see, only to the false ones, we never thought of that. The statement called out for an immediate response, such as: "How can we tell which ones are false?" But instead an awkward silence followed, and the author of the brilliant suggestion was let off the hook. It was a gem of political wisdom if ever I've heard one, and it was duly recorded by the stenographer, so there can be no denial. A line such as that will never die at the firehouse. It will be passed along for years, resurrected when trying to prove a point about city hall's wonderful insight into the fire department.

As we traveled down the darkened streets, I had to admit it was a beautiful night. The air was sweet with summer. Upon reaching Box 19, there wasn't a soul in sight. Still, we quietly scanned the area, to make sure that we weren't missing anything. The captain in charge notified headquarters, "Apparent false alarm, strike the recall." Everyone was shaking their heads, you could almost hear them say collectively, "Here we go again!" About halfway back to the station, another box began transmitting over the radio. This second box was no stranger to us either. It was located in a quiet spot on the other side of town. There was no mistaking it now, the hook-pulling nitwit was at it again. He was calling the tune for the red caravan to follow, and we traveled to our new destination like obedient robots. When we reached the box it was the same situation: no one around, apparent false alarm, strike the recall. Within seconds, another box began beeping over the radio. This one was located about a mile away. Out of respect for the sleeping citizens, we sped silently to our new destination with just our lights flashing. About this time, ten firefighters were turning into a bunch of homicidal maniacs. If our antagonist was to take the wrong corner, and run into us accidentally, he would certainly have been chased around the city by firefighters armed with pick axes, pike poles and extreme ill will. As certain as we were that the next box that came in would be a false alarm, someone would have to respond to the next location anyway. Anybody who spends enough time on the job will find that in the midst of a series of false or accidental alarms will be the real thing. So dour-faced and evil-eyed, a red caravan would wind through the city until either our nitwit nemesis decided enough was enough or until whatever fuel he was running on ran out.

Finally, the string of false alarms ended and we returned to our quarters. As we climbed the stairs to our empty bunks, the icy silence was punctuated by statements such as, "Wouldn't I like to get my hands on that maggot and strangle him!" Everyone was shaking their heads in agreement. Most of the group milled around the day room for a while before returning to their racks to salvage a little sleep. The captain, frustrated by the night's events, made what he thought was a simple statement, "Wouldn't it be great if they hid a little camera in the boxes, so when someone pulled the hook, it would take their picture?" Everyone in the room looked at him, as if he had three heads. The captain couldn't understand what was wrong with this statement, it seemed reasonable enough. In fact, it was much too reasonable. Especially for this group, that had such a proclivity for outrageous statements, even under normal conditions. In the *Cracker Factory* reasonable statements just weren't sufficient, it was time to hit that verbal overdrive that is so abundant around the firehouse.

The tiller man, Cliff Chubbuck, was a senior man and generally the most vocal when responding to an officer's opinion. He stood directly in front of the captain and stared at him in mocking disbelief.

"A picture! A picture!" he repeated in exaggerated disgust. "What do you want to do, make wallet-sized copies, Cap, so we can carry them around with us? Or do you want to make a six-by-nine glossy that we can frame and put up on the wall? Are we talking color here, Cap, or black and white?"

The captain, growing defensive now, said, "How are we going to catch this guy unless we have some evidence that captures him in the act?"

"Picture, my arse!" said Cliffy "I'd straighten him out. Put some plastic explosives in there, and when he pulls the lever, his hand would get blown off. End of story, no more problems!"

"Don't you think that's a little severe for pulling a false alarm, Cliffy?" the captain responded, as he looked around the room at the rest of the disgruntled bunch.

Of course, Cliffy wasn't going to give an inch now, so he went off on a tangent.

"No, I don't think it's too severe! Look at what the Arab countries do when they catch you stealing, they cut your hand off! That's it, no more stealing! Besides he'd still have one hand left to wipe his arse. And if he wanted to keep that one, it's simple: don't pull any more false alarms."

The captain looked around the room for some support, but there was none there. At this point, we all shared this outrageous line of reasoning. Inspired by Cliff's remarks, I added my own bit of insane logic.

"Aren't the pull stations usually located on telephone poles? And isn't there a high-voltage wire on the pole? Why couldn't we just hot wire that sucker right to the lever? That would be the end of it, there would be nothing but one charred nitwit when we got there."

The ladder driver added his two cents, "Maybe, we should

have just enough juice to blow him about forty feet from the pole. Then when we get there, we could walk over to him and say, 'Let me take a wild guess, did you just pull a false alarm or does smoke always come out of your ears?'"

The captain looked at us shaking his head, "And how are we going to be sure it isn't an innocent party we've electrocuted, who actually might have needed help?"

Cliff erupted at this, "Oh, Cap, come on! You know the same boxes get pulled every week. It is the same ones over and over. We haven't had a legitimate alarm off of one of those poles in ten years. Anyway, it's like the electric chair, once in a while you execute the wrong man. That's the justice system—it's as simple as that!"

The captain, finally realizing there wasn't a modicum of reason in the room, was the first to head back to his bunk and try to get a few hours of sleep. Without his sanity to skewer with our ludicrous comments, the rest of us decided to retire to our bunks as well.

The morning came oh-too-soon. We were all back in the day room drinking black coffee, and still talking about killing someone. Once again, the night's work was going to ruin the next day for us. If you were lucky enough to take a nap, you might reclaim the day, but most of us had things to do. So we would just have to walk around with pins and needles in our heads constantly yawning until we recovered from our sleepless night.

Inevitably, the conversations returned to false alarms and pull stations. After being burned once, it was obvious the captain would sit this one out. It started when someone said, "They ought to take all those boxes off the poles, they're a waste of time and money. For crying out loud, the only time most of them are opened is when the wire department is fixing their ancient innards because of a malfunction." Someone else chimed in, "The only place you need these boxes is in the factory areas where there are no houses to call in a fire. Everybody has a phone today. Those boxes were put there because there were no phones—that's the only reason they're there. There's a city I read about where they removed eighty percent of their boxes and sold them to collectors for a huge amount of money."

We had it all figured out before eight in the morning: sell all the boxes and save money on maintenance. It was a great idea, everyone of us nodding our heads in support, except, of course, the captain who might actually be held responsible for one of our ingenious ideas—if it was ever put into action.

We all left the station with a little satisfaction anyway, knowing we could solve the world's problems given half a chance. It was a beautiful Sunday morning, but it seemed more like an extension of Saturday night to a tired firefighter. There was no bounce at all in my step that morning. Normally, I would have headed home to read the Sunday paper while the rest of the clan slept late, but instead I had an appointment to keep. My side job was that of a furniture mover—otherwise known as a "carrier of heavy objects for money." Although the job required more knowledge than people think, it fell well short of nuclear physics.

A few days previously, I had promised an elderly woman that I would come to her home and look at an upright piano that she thought was causing her living room floor to sag. A local businessman had promised to take the piano, but then reneged on the deal, even refusing to return her calls. Frustrated, she began calling charitable organizations and retail piano stores, trying to find someone to take the piano away for free. Someone had told her that I was the local piano mover and probably knew people that would be glad to get a free upright piano. Now she felt sure that I was the one to help her with this problem. Even though the value of my assistance had been grossly exaggerated, I felt compelled to at least visit her and try to be of some help if at all possible. It would be hard to refuse an elderly woman my own feeble advice—especially after the last person she dealt with had treated her so shabbily.

Her house was in a quiet spot down by the seashore, and the air was full with the fresh smell of the ocean. Fragments of light from the brilliant morning sun seemed to follow me as I drove past the sea. It was early and the beaches were nearly empty. Normally, you couldn't buy a parking space within half a mile of the water, but now it was all parallel white lines and black pavement.

My destination turned out to be a little bungalow with a newly cut lawn. It was neat as a pin with every detail meticulously maintained, although some of the methods used would not have been my first choices. For instance, the foundation had been carefully painted. Each stone was painted in a stone-like color, and the mortar joints were done in a light gray. The brick stairs had been treated in the same fashion. Although the outcome of all this work did nothing for me, I had to admire the effort that went in to such an undertaking. At the sound of the truck door closing, a woman's head popped up from the flower garden, she was already hard at work at 8.30 a.m. on a Sunday. Walking out of the garden to greet me, she said, "You must be Mr. McCourt?" The woman was short and stocky, about seventy years of age, with a faint British accent, which I remembered from her phone call. I complimented her on the finely kept appearance of the property, so she gave me a quick tour of the premises with obvious pride. There wasn't a weed in the flower bed, or two blades of grass that weren't cut to the same height. As she led me into the house, I asked her if indeed it was a British accent I detected.

"Yes, it's true," she replied. She went on to tell me that at the end of World War II, she met an American GI, and after a brief courtship they were married. Since he was an Irish Catholic Yank, he wasn't thought of as much of a catch by his new Protestant in-laws, so they moved to the States, where there were plenty of jobs, and he could escape the wrath of her family. On the other side of the ocean, her husband's family was just glad to have him home in one piece—even with an English bride. "He was a character," she said. "He liked to drink a little, but he could charm a room-ful or stadium full, it didn't make a difference." As we walked through the house, she pointed out a photograph of the two of them, taken on their wedding day. He was tall and handsome in his dress uniform, and she looked lovely hanging on his arm, dressed in her Sunday best. For a few seconds, she just stared at the photograph, as if drawn back to a moment that took place almost fifty years before.

"You made a handsome couple," I said, breaking the silence.

"I'm afraid I'm just a fat old widow now," she laughed, and finally looked away from her cherished photo.

"Let me show you the piano, Mr. McCourt! I'm sure you have other things to do."

"No problem, ma'am," I replied. "I'm sure my wife and kids are still in bed."

The piano in question turned out to be a small upright that didn't look too heavy, but I suppose that's like saying it was a small elephant. They're all heavy, it's just a matter of how heavy. Large uprights usually run between 550 and 850 pounds. This one probably clocked in at a little under 700 pounds—surely it was nothing to cause a floor to sag. She pointed out the slant in the floor and expressed her fear that the piano had caused this situation. In her mind, something catastrophic was sure to hap-pen in the near future if the piano was not removed from the house. There was no question that the floor near the piano was uneven, so I went down to the basement to have a look at the floor joists.

After a cursory inspection, I came to the conclusion that the house was settling due to forces other than the piano. I tried to point out the real culprit of the problem, but she would have none of it. The seed had been sown already: the piano was the guilty party and had to be removed. I didn't count them at the time, but she must have had at least two dozen reasons why the piano must exit the premises, for instance: "It's a monstrosity," "Nobody has played it in years," "It won't hold a tune," "Why would I tune it if nobody plays it?" "You can't paint or wallpaper behind it, you can't even move it to dust, and you should see the dust back there!" "It blocks the natural flow of traffic between the rooms," "Some poor child could be taking lessons on it." And the list went on. I felt like joining in with a few of my own reasons, only mine would be absurd: "It looks like a dinosaur squatting in your living room," or "It would make one hell of a lawn ornament," and so on. But I just listened, knowing she needed to get this off her mind. After listening to the list of offenses that this piano was guilty of, I, too, was persuaded it had to go. If there had been another piano mover with me, we would have evicted the disgusting beast immediately. But lacking another mover, I could only agree with the course of action she had decided on, and this seemed to please her immensely.

It was time to depart. She returned to her gardening after extracting a promise from me to do whatever I could to find a home for the piano (other than hers, of course). I knew it couldn't be an idle promise, she'd been burned once by a double-talker already. His sins were going to fall on my soul if I didn't provide some honest assistance.

The ride home was enjoyable, the towns were just beginning to stir. People filing into church, buying newspapers and enjoying a fine Sunday morning. It was peaceful driving on the nearly empty roads. My eyes and thoughts could leisurely wander, without the usual congestion of traffic to occupy my attention and elevate my blood pressure. As I drove through an intersection, something caught my eye that brought me to an abrupt halt. Quickly, I pulled over to the curb. A wooden building on the other side of the street was pumping smoke. Smoke was being pushed out of every crack and crevice across the entire front of the building on the ground floor. The few people walking by were just casting curious glances as they passed. To a firefighter these outward signs were evidence of a much more serious situation developing inside the structure's walls. The pumping smoke indicated that a hidden fire was surely growing somewhere inside the first floor. The heat within was expanding the air with enough pressure to push out the hot gases wherever there was no resistance.

As I exited my truck, I took a good look at the building. It was something you would see in most cities: a commercial business on the ground level with residential units on the two upper floors. Your first instinct is to run over and pound on the doors to alert the residents of the imminent danger. As a firefighter though, I know the consequences of doing that: if the emergency personnel are not notified, then that means no help is coming. Help that has the tools and the know-how to deal with a worst-case scenario.

There was a convenience store a few doors down from where I parked. I ran inside and told the cashier I needed a phone immediately to call the fire department because the building across the street was on fire. Unfortunately, there was a language barrier.

The people who owned the store were Asian, and I'm not sure if they had a phone or didn't have a phone or were just suspicious of my motives since no building was visibly on fire. "No phone! No phone!" was the only response I received. There was no time to debate the issue, I raised my voice and said, "Then tell me where the fire alarm is, so I can pull it!" As I demonstrated the act of pulling a box, to hopefully overcome the language barrier. They pointed to a telephone pole that couldn't have been more than twenty feet from the front of the building. I ran out and sure enough there was a pull station on the pole, and for the first time in my life, I dropped the hook. Then I ran as fast as I could to the front of the burning building, knowing that time was of the essence.

As I reached the building, a door that led to the upper floors opened, and people began staggering out disoriented and coughing. The stairway had already begun to fill with smoke. I moved them away from the front of the building, where the hidden fire on the first floor was quickly growing. In the distance, the sound of sirens could be heard already. Even as an active member of the fire department, it still amazed me how quickly the engines were dispatched. Suddenly, a large window on the first floor exploded, sending glass across the sidewalk. This self-venting would surely lead to a quick expansion of the fire. I turned to the residents who were still choking from the smoke trying to understand what was going on. I grabbed one of the adults by the arm and asked him if everyone was out of the building. He quickly looked around and said, "I think so." Not releasing my grip, I said, "Look again, we have to be sure." Hearing the urgency in my voice, he turned and took a head count and said, "Yeah, everyone is out," which was music to my ears. I certainly didn't want to scale those stairs unless it was absolutely necessary and I didn't want firefighters arriving on the scene to get the wrong information and risk their lives for people who had already exited the building.

The station the engine was coming from wasn't too far away, more than once my own Engine 3 had been sent there to cover on mutual aid. Looking in that direction, I could see the engine approaching and hear the air horn blaring. When the engine pulled up next to the building, the flames from the first-floor window were already extending up past the second-floor window. As a firefighter, I'm biased when it comes to the fire service, but in all honesty, it took maybe a shade over two minutes from the time I pulled the hook till the time the first piece arrived. The engine had a four-man crew: a lieutenant, a pump operator, and two firefighters. As the lieutenant donned his air tank, he yelled to the two firefighters, "Get me the two-and-a-half-inch line off the rear." I told him that there was a hydrant across the street and if he wanted I would dress it and lay a length of hose to his pump. With all the self-assurance of a true professional, he looked me in the face and said, "That won't be necessary, sir, we have another pump on the way, and they'll be laying us a line. Thanks anyway." He did the right thing. Firefighters depend on the men they work with, if they let a stranger get involved, that would only be asking for trouble.

The firefighters had the line ready and called for the water. The pump operator was a younger man, who didn't look as if he had been to many fires—even his turn-out gear was fairly new. In firefighter lingo, it looked as if he'd barely got his boots wet yet. He looked at the pump panel with all its dials, gauges and gates, then reached out and stopped as if an invisible force was holding him. He was drawing a complete blank. I asked him if he had flipped the switch in the cab to put it into pump. He nodded his head quickly "Yes," but still looked panic-stricken.

I told him, "Pull your tank to pump," then I ran to the back of the pump and yelled back, "Open gate number three." He responded instantly and the water began to flow. As I walked past him, he gave me a heartfelt thanks. Smiling, I said, "I know the feeling." The same thing happens to every pump operator at one time or another—and more than once to yours truly. For the first few minutes of a fire, the pump operator's job can be hectic. After that, it is probably the most boring job on the department. The lieutenant struck a second alarm on the box, and the air was full with sirens. It was time to leave. I didn't want anyone confusing me with some sparky who chases fires when they're not on duty.

As I drove home, I breathed in the soft, sweet air again. It lulled me with its comfort, it seemed a long time since my morning cup of coffee at the station. The prominent role I played in the invective-filled tirade about pull stations, seemed ironic to me now. If the exit in that building had been blocked by fire, that pullbox might have been the only possible chance of salvation for those people. I knew I would tell everyone at the station the following week about the fire and the first hook I ever dropped, but I definitely wouldn't get on the soapbox in support of fire alarm boxes. No, the story would speak for itself—and very well, I might add. Promoting fire boxes would only set me up for the same abuse that the captain had received the previous night. Besides everyone needed to vent their frustrations anyway, even if there was nothing that they could do about it. It was time to go home, grab a few sections of the Sunday paper, take them into the bedroom and close the door. Then after perusing the paper for a while, perhaps I could fall asleep and reclaim the day from the hook-pulling nitwit who had stolen it from me the night before.

A few weeks later, I traveled the same route as that Sunday morning. The only reminders of what happened that day were some boarded-up windows, a long black singe mark that ran up the front of the building and a few neatly patched holes in the roof. The structure was still fully intact, in fact, it was a great stop.

I had just picked up an upright piano from a woman with a British accent who couldn't have been happier to see it go. In her mind, I think the house actually straightened itself a little as the piano went out the door. A family with two young children was really excited about getting an instrument in such good condition. Now, there were different phrases being bandied about, such as: "They don't make them like this anymore," "Oh wow, real ivory keys," and "Look at the mahogany wood and the carvings on the case." The piano's stock had soared in its new home. It was a classic example of something seldom used that still was useful in the right situation. The telephone pole pullboxes and the old upright pianos were slowly headed toward extinction, but until then, they would serve a purpose. There was definitely one firefighter, who wouldn't be so vocal the next time the group was bashing pull stations and electrocuting nitwits.

Protection of Life and Property

I N MOST TYPES OF business, there are certain measure-
ments for success or failure. If a real estate agent sells more
properties than anyone else in their office, they become the
top agent. If a branch manager's store sales are more than all the
others, he is regarded as the most productive. Did you meet your
deadline? Is the quality of the finished product acceptable? The
answers to those questions mean everything in business.

In firefighting, it's a different story. If you save half of a
structure from being destroyed by fire, did you do a good job? If
you respond to a medical emergency quickly and professionally,
but the patient dies, can it be called a success? How can you ever
know how well your fire department is performing, when success
is measured in degrees of loss rather than by gain? In the fog of
this uncertainty, every decision plays an important role. Yet the
mission is simple: protection of life and property.

On the sidewalk, with a sheepish look on his face, stood a
young boy of about nine or ten years of age. Two engines, a ladder

and the rescue had been summoned by the activation of the fire-box, which was mounted on a telephone pole directly adjacent to the boy. A quick look around told us that nothing at the scene would warrant a full box assignment. The captain climbed out of Engine 1 to see what had happened, while the rest of us sat in the apparatus awaiting the outcome.

The boy seemed a little overwhelmed by it all. Four large trucks had come speeding down the street with sirens blaring, red lights flashing, and now a dozen faces were staring down on the lad in expectation. He looked rather small standing there in the midst of it all. The captain approached him with his head cocked in a quizzical way, and asked the obvious question, "Did you pull the hook in this firebox, son?" The boy hesitated for a moment, then nodded his head in assent. "Why?" the captain asked. Under the scrutiny of all this attention, the boy seemed to lose his tongue for a moment. Then in a voice inaudible to anyone but the captain, he told his story.

He had been heading home after playing with friends when suddenly he was confronted by a large angry dog. The dog was barking and growling in a manner that had scared the hell out of him. The boy said he tried to get away but couldn't, so when he saw the pull station it seemed like a good way to get help. The captain took a look around and then asked the boy, "Where is the dog now?" The boy told him that the dog had bolted at the sound of the engines coming down the street.

The captain didn't seem satisfied with the explanation, but he just shook his head and warned the boy not to touch the fire alarm boxes in the future unless there was a real emergency. To most of us, the boy's explanation seemed logical. Why would the kid pull the hook and then wait for us to show up if it was a false alarm? Regardless, the captain gave him a quick lecture about tying up so many firefighters when someone else might really need help in another part of the city, and then sent the little guy on his way. After the lecture, he instructed the dispatcher to, "Strike the recall, false alarm, all companies are returning to quarters." A phrase you hear countless times if you're in the firefighting business.

So the two engines, a ladder truck and the rescue retraced their routes back to their stations. One of the pumps and the ladder truck were over twenty years old, but because we kept each one shined and the body styles changed so seldom, a civilian would have no way of knowing that their first-response vehicles would soon become antiques. In fact, some of us on the job liked the old trucks better than the newer ones, so we didn't complain too much about the old warhorses.

At headquarters, the engine, ladder and rescue would return from a false alarm at the same time. There would always be a flurry of activity around the apparatus as everyone took off their gear before heading back upstairs after a run. As the group milled around and straightened things out for the next run, one of the senior men spoke up to the captain, "Hey, Cap, can I ask you a question? What did the kid do that was wrong?" Everybody stopped talking and looked over at the captain waiting for a response. When a senior man threw out a question like that with all ears in attendance, you knew something was up.

The captain looked at him a little puzzled and said, "What are you talking about? You don't call in a box over a growling dog!" The senior man considered the captain's response for a moment and then asked him another question.

"What's the definition of a firefighter's mission as it's written in the job description?" He didn't wait but a second for an answer then he added, "protection of life and property, that's what it is, and as far as that kid knew his life was being threatened."

Looking to deflect the criticism that caught him by surprise, the captain reiterated, "You don't send two engines, a ladder and a rescue over a growling dog!"

"Well, you can tell his parents that, if they come down and complain about what you told their son, and as far as I remember we were all sitting on our asses when the box came in." The senior man turned and went upstairs, leaving the captain mumbling something to himself as he walked up to his office without another word.

It was a good example of a senior man assuming a leadership role regardless of rank. It was a gray area and opinions were voiced. None of us wanted a bunch of ten year olds dropping hooks all over the city and then claiming that their lives were in jeopardy, but none of us wanted some little kid getting hurt because he was afraid to touch a firebox either. We would have rather the captain just ask the boy if he was all right, pat him on the head and maybe add, "Remember only in emergencies," then send him on his way with no guilt over the incident. Sometimes, it's that simple, other times it's much more complex.

The "sleeper trick," that's what they called watching the desk between the hours of 2.00 p.m. and 4.00 p.m. in the afternoon. At headquarters, a firefighter was assigned to answer the phone and respond to radio transmissions (at that mess we called a "communications center"). It was known as being the houseman. And from 8.00 a.m. to 9.00 p.m. each day, firefighters would take a turn at watching the desk for the real houseman who would slide down the pole to take over the job whenever we responded to a call. It's called the sleeper trick because after lunch, if the radio and phones were quiet, the man working the desk would get a bad case of whiplash as he tried to keep from falling out of the chair while struggling to keep his eyes open. At times when the phone rang during one of these spells, it would be like a bolt of lightning shooting through your brain.

This particular day, I was working the dreaded sleeper trick, and the time couldn't have been going by slower unless I was being tortured. The countless cable channels on the television were a waste of the city's money. I had already read the newspaper, and the daily special that we had enjoyed a little while ago at lunch was acting like a narcotic as I struggled to keep my eyes open.

When the phone rang, I nearly fell out of my chair. As I reached over in a fog to answer it, I noticed it was the emergency line, which helped clear out some of the cobwebs real quick. I grabbed a pencil as I picked up the phone, hoping it was one of the many non-emergency calls that somehow manage to come in on the hot line, but the minute I heard the woman's voice I knew that wasn't the case.

"Please send the rescue my husband has shot himself!" The woman's voice was shaking with emotion. "What's the address?" I asked, knowing how critical that piece of information could become if for some reason the conversation ended prematurely. Back then, there was no little magic box that displayed the address automatically, and when the situation is drastic sometimes a caller is unable to relay even the most basic information.

She told me the street address and I repeated it back to her, as always, to be sure there was no mistake. The location wasn't a long run from headquarters if the traffic allowed the rescue a little room to maneuver. Then I asked her where the wound was located.

"In his head," she replied, then added, "Please hurry!"

"Ma'am, I'm dispatching the rescue right now, they'll be there in a few minutes."

"Hurry!" she said again as the conversation ended.

"Attention, attention, the rescue company, please respond to a man down with a gunshot wound to the head." In what seemed like an instant, the rescue crew had slid down the poles and climbed into the truck. After I confirmed the address with them, they were on their way. As they left the building, I expected the captain to call down and instruct me to send Engine 2 to assist them, since E2 was situated right around the corner from the location of the call. A few seconds later, the direct line from the captain's office rang. It wasn't the captain, though, instead it was the lieutenant and after he confirmed the address, he told me the devastating news: the house belonged to one of our own firefighters.

It was a shock. The victim now had a familiar face and that always made matters worse. I immediately asked the lieutenant if I could dispatch Engine 2 to assist at the scene. As I listened, the lieutenant said, "Cap, Doug wants to dispatch Engine 2 to the scene." There was a moment of hesitation, before I heard the reply. "If they need an engine, they'll call for one." I couldn't imagine why he would object to sending some extra help, but at the time it was standard procedure to initially only send the rescue. Two men answering a call for a gunshot wound to the head? As someone who had worked the rescue, it didn't seem like enough to me.

I stood by the radio waiting to hear from the rescue company. After a few minutes, they made their first report, "Rescue is off at the scene." Then less than a minute later, another terse transmission. "Rescue to Melrose Fire, send an engine company down here to assist!" Engine 2 was almost out the door before

I dispatched them, they had been listening to the rescue's call for help as well and expected the request for assistance.

It wasn't long before Engine 2 called over the radio, "Engine 2 is off at the scene assisting the rescue company." As I waited at the desk for another update, I remembered working with the firefighter who was now fighting for his life. During a conversation, we had found out that both of our wives were in the last trimester of their pregnancies. It was hard to imagine the desperate scene that was taking place as I sat there lost in thought, listening for their next report. It was bad enough to be dealing with a gunshot wound to the head of a fellow firefighter, but to have his pregnant wife present during such a horrible mess just made it that much worse.

After a brief radio silence, that seemed like an eternity, the rescue called in again. "Melrose Rescue to Melrose Fire, the Rescue and Engine 2 are transporting a patient to the hospital." All I could do was acknowledge receiving the message. Now everyone would have to wait until they returned to quarters to learn the outcome. A somber silence fell over the station. I thought of my buddy Dick Crowell who was part of the rescue crew that day. Was there any way he would ever miss one of these brutal calls? He always managed to end up on every gut-wrenching medical aid. It was so uncanny that we started calling him "Lucky," in a true display of the black humor found at the firehouse.

After what seemed like a long time, the rescue was on the air again. "Melrose Rescue to Melrose Fire, Engine 2 and the Rescue are returning in service." When they returned to the station both of them looked thoroughly drained—almost as if they'd aged a few years in that brief span of time. For a few moments, there was an uncomfortable silence until someone asked what everyone wanted to know. "Did he make it?" The answer, unfortunately, was no.

He had been alive when they got there, but it was a devastating wound to his head. After they called for an engine company, the two of them tried to deal with the wound, but in the end the damage was just too great. Someone asked Dickie if the wife was there the whole time. All he could say was that it was, "horrible, a real mess," and I could see the worry lines etched in his face. Dick was a single parent and sometimes after a bad call there was no one there to talk to at home. As we stood there talking, I knew that later on that night I'd drop by his house with a few beers and try to help—that is, if empathy and an attentive ear could be of any help.

Evidently, the gun had accidentally discharged as he was putting it away in a place that was out of reach. After talking to Dick, I really think our friend would have died no matter how many companies responded to the scene that day. Although having said that, the rescue company and the wife of our fellow firefighter all suffered more than they should have, and really without good reason. The crew of Engine 2 would have probably arrived on the scene before the rescue. There would have been extra hands to do the running for the EMTs, while they were working on the patient, as well as someone to help this distraught woman through one of the most stressful situations of her life.

Eventually, an engine company would be assigned to almost every medical aid because of these types of situations. Yet something tells me a general order shouldn't have been necessary. "Protection of life and property," it's a simple description, but one that's almost poetic. It has led countless firefighters into harm's way while trying to achieve those noble goals. Whether the call is for a burning building, a medical aid or just a young boy trying to escape the wrath of an angry dog, it's all protection of life and property. And when you see it in that light there are no gray areas.

A Good Place to Hide

S OMETIMES THE SLOW DAYS at the firehouse were the worst. Especially when I was young, and idle time seemed like such a waste. A quiet day in the station could seem like a week to a young man full of energy, so my main objective would be to find ways to amuse myself. This particular day was a prime example and I would never have remembered it, if it wasn't for a certain phrase uttered by a fellow firefighter.

There were twelve of us on the shift and I was making the rounds trying to kill time. Maybe, if I was lucky, I could get Dave to elaborate on his time spent serving under General Patton in World War II. Or perhaps Carl would tell me again what it was like eating sand at Iwo Jima as enemy snipers waited for a clean shot. Oh, there were plenty of stories at the firehouse besides those in the firefighting war chest. There were sailors who served at Midway, and my pal Danny from the wire department who served as a medic with the Marines when the crap was really hitting the fan in Korea. After all, the fire department gives preference to veterans, so we were well-stocked with representatives of several wars. They never talked much about the blood and gore, but they all held strong opinions as to what they had seen.

Despite having all these witnesses to many of the most dramatic moments in the twentieth century, on this day, for some reason, the historians were all mute. When this happened, my next option would be to seek out someone who was just plain entertaining. Some character whose very nature seemed to provoke a few smiles. We had one senior member who fit the description perfectly. My job would be to track him down and hopefully elicit a positive response. His name was Cliffy, which was short for Clifford, although I never heard a single soul call him Clifford. He was a rather large man with a partially bald head ringed by silver. He always carried a pocket watch and would look at it through his wire-rimmed glasses like a train conductor. At first glance, he looked as straight as an arrow, but he was a comedian who looked at everything a little differently.

Finding him should have been an easy enough task—after all, we were all trapped inside the same four brick walls. First, I checked the dispatch office to see if he might be taking his turn at answering the phones. In the station, it was known as *pulling a trick*, but he wasn't there and hadn't been seen. Next, I checked out the television room without success, and nobody was conscious enough to answer any of my missing person questions. Then it was up to the third floor to scout out the gym and the few chairs facing the windows where some of the crew did a little reading. Nothing. So I went back to the first floor and worked my way up to the third floor once again with the same results. Again, nothing. Now he had managed to pique my imagination—where the hell was he? I checked the bathroom, then the bedrooms to see if he was trying to sneak a nap. Then I tried the cellar, but it was as dark as a tomb. Well, at least I had found something to occupy my time: tracking down a missing Group 4 constituent.

This was no accident: he was making himself scarce on purpose and my mission was to find him. As to why I felt compelled to do this, I have no idea. Mindless boredom, I suppose. I wandered by the chief's office and the captain's office, then I checked out the area in front of the station and behind the station. Nothing. It was turning into a real mystery. He had been known to do this occasionally in the past. Even to the point where he would refuse to answer a voice page over the loudspeaker, because he knew it was really only idle curiosity as to his whereabouts. There was a pool table on the second floor and off to the side of the room was a door that led to an old wooden porch on top of our dispatch office. It was probably the only place in the entire building that I hadn't checked, so I went over and opened the door to take a peek. Nothing, but as I turned to walk away I remembered that there was an alcove in the farthest corner of the porch. I opened the door and walked out on to the porch until I could see into the alcove. Well, lo and behold! There he was sitting on a wooden chair tucked away into that hidden recess, with his feet propped up on the old decrepit railing.

"Well, there you are!" I exclaimed. "I've been looking all over the station for you."

"Really," he replied, "Why, what's up?"

Feeling somewhat foolish now I said, "Nothing, I'm just bored and I hadn't seen you all afternoon. I never thought to look out here."

"It's a good place to hide," he replied with a sly grin on his face.

"Hide from what?" I asked not knowing what he meant.

"Oh, from a lot of things," he said with conviction. "Every station should have a good place to hide."

He shot me an ironic smile. He seemed to enjoy the absurdity of the statement. Then he proceeded to educate me on the best places to hide in each of the Melrose stations. I sat on the railing thoroughly enjoying his explanations, no longer bored. Mission accomplished.

At that stage of my career, I felt trapped on a slow day in the station. The same four walls along with the interminably slow passage of the hours while on duty, seemed suffocating to my youthful spirit. Yet as time went by, I found myself seeking out that alcove on the porch more and more. Sometimes, to get away from the rest of the crew when things got argumentative, and sometimes, just for a peaceful place to be alone with my thoughts. At home, I now had two children and all the responsibilities that come with raising a family. There was always something to do and if you were sitting idly, it was because the to-do list was being ignored. So it wasn't often that I had a chance to sit quietly by myself without some obligation pressuring me into action.

Sometimes, it felt good to sit out on the old porch, if only to smell the fresh air. Away from the damp, mildew stench of the rotting lengths of canvas fire hose. Away from the smoky stench of firefighters' gear that still reeked from a recent fire. All those familiar smells that, if you close your eyes, say firehouse. Away from the engine bay where the sound of water dripping from a leaky tank is as constant as a clock. It makes you wonder why metal was ever chosen to hold the five hundred gallons carried in the old pump. Away from the voices on the scanners jumping through the air at unsuspecting moments, breaking your train of thought and the silent bells that are always present, ready to turn a dull atmosphere upside down at any moment.

Someone could lead you in here blindfolded and in one quiet moment you'd know you're at the firehouse and there would be a grain of comfort in that realization. For to be there means you're not out at some tragedy trying to make things right. Trying to put the pieces of some alien puzzle back together only to find out some of them are missing. Yes, there were times after a particularly dramatic call had temporarily rattled your nerves that you needed a good place to hide.

A voice spoke to me in a dream, "Attention, attention, rescue company respond to a possible suicide." Something was shining in my eyes as I wrestled with the blankets in the bed. Then a different voice called out a few seconds later, "Did you get that, Doug, there's a call for the rescue company." It wasn't a dream at all. I had managed to remain unconscious through the tone alert and the vocal announcement over the intercom, as well as the house lights shining in my face. Usually, I never slept that soundly in the firehouse, but sometimes in a rare moment of deep sleep everything would transpire as in a dream.

As soon as I realized that it was an actual call, I was out of the bed like a bolt, and sliding down the pole a bit too fast while trying to shake the cobwebs from my head. There were thick rubber cushions at the foot of each pole that acted as shock absorbers for those occasions when the brass pole seemed to be coated with a thin layer of slippery oil. Fortunately, as we sped through the nearly empty streets that night, my partner Dave was driving. At times, he was a little bit of a speed demon when he was at the wheel of the rescue truck, which was the fastest vehicle used by the fire department. This particular time, it was a good thing because being in fear for my life brought me quickly to my senses.

The address to which we were responding was a long run from our station. It was a little dead-end street, right on the edge of town. As we made the final turn on to the street, I realized it was one of the few streets in the city that I had never been on before. Driving down the street, I scanned the houses with the spotlight trying to catch a number. Those four-inch-tall house numbers don't exactly jump out at you in the black of night. It's always a good idea after dialing 911 to snap on the front entrance light, because at three or four in the morning it might very well be the only one lit on the street, which would make our job a lot easier. But, understandably, in the emotional chaos of the moment sometimes this was overlooked.

As luck would have it, the house we were looking for was the very last one on the street. This house was different than any of the others on the street. All the rest appeared to be modest single family homes, but this one had been altered and now it stood head and shoulders above the rest. It definitely gave you the impression that the owners of the house had prospered in recent times. Besides being twice the size of any other on the street, there were also a pair of luxury vehicles in the driveway. The call was for a suicide, I reminded myself. It seemed prosperity hadn't brought peace of mind along to keep it company.

We were met at the door by a woman who probably was in her mid-fifties. She was obviously upset but was trying hard to keep her composure. As we followed her through the house, she told us that the victim was her daughter and that she had been living here with her daughter's family. Evidently, her daughter and son in-law had been having marital problems and the family physician had prescribed some medication for her daughter to deal with the stress. Her daughter had been quite upset earlier in the night and went to her room saying she wanted to be alone for a while. When the mother awoke in the middle of the night and heard the television in her daughter's room was still on, she decided to peek in the room just to check on her. If for no other reason than to lend some emotional support.

The woman was telling us the name of the medication as we finally entered the bedroom after a circuitous trip through the spacious house. My first impression was that it looked more like a movie set than it did an emergency rescue scene. It was an enormous, tastefully decorated room and lying on a large bed was an attractive woman dressed in a white satin nightgown. As we walked over to check her condition, I thought to myself perhaps the scene was staged and she really just wanted attention—it wouldn't have been the first time. From what I had seen in the past, suicide scenes usually didn't look like this. Instead, the victim might look like they were dead drunk with some vomit leaking out of the corner of their mouth—an ugly mess, to say the least. Yet here she was looking like a make-up artist had just finished touching her up for the final scene.

Dave proceeded to take her blood pressure and record the vitals, while I set up the portable oxygen. He nodded to me after he finished obtaining the numbers and said, "She definitely took something!" As my partner hooked up our patient to the oxygen, I went out to get the cot because it was an obvious transport. By now, my blood pressure and pulse rate were heading upwards. How much of the drug had she taken? Hopefully not enough to cause permanent damage or death. Let's get her to the hospital, I thought to myself, before something unexpected happens. It would be a real horror show if we ended up doing CPR to this young woman right in front of her mother.

We had her up and on the cot in two seconds, she couldn't have weighed more than 110 pounds. After strapping her to the cot, we were on our way in no time; not many of our transports went that easy. Dave was the chauffeur so he would call in a report to the hospital, while I stayed in back and monitored the condition of our patient. The poor mother was left to babysit the sleeping children, while trying to make arrangements to get to the hospital.

Whenever I attended an unconscious victim on a ride to the ER, I would keep one hand on their wrist to check the radial pulse, while also watching their chest to keep track of the respirations.

The young woman in front of me was breathing, but just barely. After a few moments, I heard the sound of the intercom being activated by my partner. Glancing in the rearview mirror, Dave had noticed me intently watching the woman. She looked like the princess who had taken a bite out of the poisoned apple and fallen asleep. After a moment's hesitation, he said, "Don't get any funny ideas, Firefighter McCourt." He was trying to insinuate that it wasn't just her respirations that I had on my mind, as I focused on our patient's breathing. Sometimes, you forget that outrageous statements are considered an art form on this job. When I glanced into the rearview mirror with a disgusted look, he smirked as if to say, "Gotcha!"

It was typical firefighter form and I should have seen it coming, but actually I wasn't thinking that at all. What was really going on inside my head was, how did an attractive young woman who lived in the biggest house on her street end up as an attempted suicide case in the back of our rescue? Perhaps, only a few shallow breaths away from leaving this world. It's one thing to read about it in the newspaper, but to see something like this unfold before your eyes, well, it leaves you shaking your head and wondering, "Why?"

It was a strange feeling sitting there holding her hand as I watched her faintly breathing. It was hard to see someone try to cut their life so short, when they appeared to be so blessed. Yet, early on in firefighting, I had learned that this job presented you with questions to which there were no answers. All we could do was try to help save her life and hope that if she survived she would appreciate the effort, rather than regret it. When we turned our patient over to the staff at the ER, I felt good about her chances of recovery. I tried not to do follow-ups on the patients that we brought to the hospital. If we hadn't done our job right, the folks in the ER would certainly let us know, otherwise, as far as I knew, they were still alive. It was a defense mechanism of sorts, I suppose.

While Dave did the paperwork and chatted with a staff member, I rolled the cot down the hall to change the sheets and get ready to return to the station. It was quiet at the hospital at three o'clock in the morning, even some of the lights were turned down low in the area where the fresh linens were stored. As I cleaned and dressed the cot, I became aware of some muffled voices, although barely audible. They were coming from a room diagonally across the hall from me. I moved over a few feet to look into the room because there seemed to be no other activity in the entire area.

There on the edge of an examination table sat a small boy with his legs dangling over the side. He was maybe five or six years old and had a face as round as an apple, with just enough baby fat to make him look like a real cute kid. A man in a white jacket, who was part of the hospital staff, was standing by his side patting the boy on the back trying to console him. The poor boy's head had no hair, either from being shaved clean or from some treatment he had endured. His chin was practically resting on his bare chest. His eyes were cast down towards the floor in sad resignation. Tears filled his eyes and streamed down his face as he wrestled with his emotions.

The man was wiping his tears with a white cloth and with a reassuring hand he kept patting the boy on the back. At that moment, barely a word was being said, yet the man's good intentions seemed to speak eloquently. It was one of those real moments, where one heart speaks and another listens. I couldn't help but think of the young woman we had just taken to the hospital. She seemed to have everything going for her and yet could find no reason to go on living. On the other hand, the young boy seemed to want nothing more than to live a normal life. If there was anything I could have done to help the boy, I surely would have, but all I could really do was go back to dressing the cot and at least give him some privacy. It's an agonizing thing to watch a child that young suffer, especially when you have children at home the same age. Sometimes, firefighting is an emotionally complicated job. It can remind you with a jolt as to what's really important in life.

As we drove back to the station, the boy and the woman consumed my thoughts. Occasionally, the job would confront me with a situation to which my mind could find no resolution. Upon returning to the station, I went to the day room to read a newspaper to try to clear my head. I waited for my body to give me some signal that it was time to go to sleep, but this time my mind stayed wide awake. The night's events had left a bright light burning in my head. As if my mind was working overtime trying to understand everything it had seen.

Eventually, I sought out the refuge of the chair in the alcove of the old wooden porch. It was peaceful sitting there above the nearly deserted streets in the middle of the night like some kind of hidden sentinel. Gazing down at the umbrellas of light cast beneath the bowed heads of the lampposts. Facing the large stone church that sits across from the station. At that moment, the silent structure seemed like a sanctuary. Its bell tower rising into the night with only an occasional breeze whispering around its darkened steeple. My comrade had been right: it was a good place to hide.

Liquid Tales

S UCCESS HAS A HUNDRED fathers but failure is an orphan (or so the saying goes), but at the firehouse we add a twisted spin to this old adage. If no one gets hurt in the process, we own the bragging rights to any debacle—no matter how foolish it may make us appear. For instance, you may have been careless enough to let your helmet fall off the engine while responding to a call, but another firefighter compounds your mistake by running over it with the ladder truck while following the engine to the same call. Unlike the real world, instead of arguing over whose at fault, the firefighters argue over who will be given credit for the leather wafer, which will surely become a trophy of sorts.

Why do we do this, you may ask? Well, it's really a matter of survival. If a person outwardly shows the rest of the group that something bothers them, then they will surely be tortured over it. I think that's actually mandatory protocol, so we're only obeying some ancient law. There is a very practical reason as well. Every mistake you make on this particular job is almost always witnessed, sometimes by dozens of people, so denial is usually out of the question. In order to survive, you must learn that nothing stems a stream of ridicule faster than when the intended target appears to be enjoying the attention, perhaps even actually a bit proud of the alleged folly. Human nature dictates that if someone enjoys torturing you, then they will cease the process if their efforts seem to produce happiness instead of pain. So Darwin was right in this instance, due to some bizarre evolutionary process a thick-skinned firefighter eventually emerged—one that was not so easily embarrassed. As a result, a good story is always worth more than your injured pride around the firehouse.

I was at a family get-together one day after a night in the station, a night that had involved working a two-alarm fire in the wee hours of the morning. The get-together was one of those children's birthday parties where all the youngsters run around, out of control, screaming like banshees. Due to the effects of my sleep deprivation, at times the screams felt like I was sticking a finger in an electrical outlet. Hot coffee was keeping me awake, but it wasn't helping my nerves at all. I found myself standing there glassy-eyed from lack of sleep, wondering if the hands on the clock had stopped, leaving me in some sort of hellish time warp.

Sooner or later, the men in our family will gravitate to a corner at this type of event to escape the chaos of the festivities. In this case, the corner I sought out was the one that put the most distance between myself and the screaming banshees. In the background, you could hear comments from the women, such as, "Doesn't that look adorable," or "Don't worry if it doesn't fit I have the receipts for it." So generally this would be the time we'd try to find a common denominator that we could talk about such as sports or the fire department. Since I had fresh material from the night before, I cornered my brother, Dave, and proceeded to tell him some of the more interesting aspects of the previous night's fire.

The fire involved your standard wood frame house. A second alarm had been struck, primarily because we were running short handed, which seemed at times to be the norm rather than the exception. I told Dave how the house had been fully charged with smoke and that the group had done a great job in stopping the fire. It was the most you could hope for when called to a house fire in the middle of the night. A good stop, with no injuries and a minimal amount of damage from the fire, although the excessive smoke had done a considerable amount of harm. But this wasn't the story, nobody wants to hear about the good stop you made the night before—that's your job, that's what you get paid to do. This was just my way of establishing the setting for the other nonsense that transpired while we were on the scene.

The fire had started in a kitchen wall on the first floor. It extended up into the wall of the second floor, which was also a kitchen since it was a two family, but we managed to stop it before it reached the attic. This was a real plus for us, because working a house fire can be nasty, but when you're forced to get up into the attic to fight it, things can get a lot nastier. In some of them, there are no floorboards so just moving around can be treacherous. Most of the time, there's not enough overhead, so you can never stand up straight. By the time you're finished with an attic fire, you have a sore back and a new world record for how many times a person can hit their head on roof rafters, which are always hidden in the smoke.

A quick response coupled with some good firefighting had kept the damage from the blaze to a minimum. All that remained was to open up all areas the fire had traveled in while it extended upwards from the first floor, into the room above it, making sure nothing was left to smolder. When firefighters work a fire such as this, you always have to remember that it's a home and not just some structure. When you leave, somebody has to deal with the mess that's left behind. So when we chase the remaining embers down at a fire, we try to use as little water as possible, because whether something is destroyed by water or fire, it's still destroyed.

There are times when you can't get enough water on a fire, but there are also times when the group has made a good stop and more water isn't needed. The last thing you want to do is ruin your efforts by causing even more damage with the reckless use of water. For example, everyone's heard of people that have been smoking in a bed only to fall asleep and accidentally set the house on fire. This particular type of fire can cause an excessive amount of smoke, so when entering a situation like that it can be very deceptive as to what is the actual source of the problem. A smoldering overstuffed chair might cause as much smoke as a raging inferno that's trapped inside the walls. The damage resulting from these situations may vary greatly depending on the methods used to fight the fire. Usually, with a smoldering mattress or chair, we'd use just enough water to knock down any active flame and then, if possible, we'd remove the item from the building entirely. This would enable us to drown the remaining fire outside the premises while also removing the cause of the smoke as well. Therefore, saving someone's home from the damage that might take place if we did the rest of our overhauling indoors.

On the other hand, what if we were to attack a situation such as this like raging bulls? We could clean out a couple of windows with an ax to relieve some of the smoke, then chop a two-foot-square hole in the roof for ventilation and drown the mattress with a few hundred gallons of water. Since most bedrooms in a house are on the second floor, a good amount of the water would eventually find its way downstairs, to boot. Imagine the difference in the amount of damage left behind for the owners in these two scenarios. Well, that's what confronts them when we leave. So new recruits and eager beavers need to be reminded: yes, we are here to put out the fire because that's definitely a priority, but our actual job description is "protection of life and property," not destroying it. This probably sounds simple enough to a civilian, but inside a building filled with smoke, with your adrenaline flowing, it's easy to get caught up in the moment and do thousands of dollars' worth of damage over a nickel's worth of fire. I can't speak for anyone else, but for my part, at the end of the day, I would hope the fire did more damage than the firefighters.

Anyway, there we were in a kitchen on the second floor, opening up a wall, cleaning out the remaining embers of the fire, trying to make sure we wouldn't be making an encore performance later in the day. We had exhausted our air tanks a long time ago, but the fire was out and we had enough doors and windows opened to reduce the smoke conditions to an acceptable level. There's a little streak of macho nonsense that runs through the firefighting world and to leave the building now for a new air tank, with this low level of smoke, would be an invitation for endless verbal abuse from the remaining firefighters. For God's sake, some of the old timers still thought the air tanks were only for sissies. Of course, they were a little out in left field, but that didn't matter when your pride was getting shredded at the firehouse. So I'd overhaul the rest of the fire without a new air tank, even though it was the equivalent of sucking down a couple of packs of cigarettes, but in some twisted way my manhood would remain intact.

There were four of us in the room, so while two firefighters worked at opening the wall, the other two could rest while using their hand lights to illuminate the job at hand. When it was my turn to hold the hand light I noticed there was a refrigerator right next to me, which I immediately opened to see if a cold beverage might be hiding in there. Perhaps there might be something to cool the fire that was beginning to burn in my throat from the acrid smoke. A cold beverage definitely would have no effect on your manhood. In fact, at the firehouse, I believe it enhances it. As I peered into the darkened interior of the refrigerator the only word that came to mind was *bingo!* There must have been a case and a half of beer, as well as, an assortment of sodas. The firefighting gods had smiled upon us. Every firefighter knows that refrigerators are made of metal and have tremendous insulating qualities, so despite a fire burning in the same room the beverages inside were still cold. The three other firefighters turned around in unison to see what elicited my unexpected exclamation. From the looks on their faces, everyone seemed to be as impressed as yours truly. After a brief discussion, we decided that the homeowner definitely would not begrudge the firefighters, who had just saved his home from ruination, a chance to obtain the therapeutic benefit of the remedies displayed before us. Sometimes in firefighting, you need to make split-second decisions and we were up to the task. It certainly would make the work more enjoyable, and since two men were resting while the other two men pulled plaster, it would work out beautifully.

A few minutes later, we heard some sounds emanating from the back stairs, which were located on the other side of the kitchen. After a few seconds, we realized it must be some firefighters trying to find an entrance to the second floor to locate the source of the smoke. I'm sure from outside of the building it probably appeared as if there was still more fire on the inside, but in reality all that was left was some smoke and a few hot spots that needed to be exposed. I heard a voice in the stairway say,

"I found it, Lieutenant," followed by the sound of the doorknob turning at the other end of the room. The door popped open and in crawled a firefighter. He was from another city and he didn't have an air tank on so he was choking from all the smoke trapped in the back stairwell. He could barely see out of his burning eyes as he tried to survey the room. Then he began to crawl forward. I believe, he thought the yellow glow from our hand lights was actually a source of fire. He called back over his shoulder, "Over here, Lieu, I think I found it." We were all standing there watching him crawl across the floor and listening to his fellow firefighters stumbling in the stairwell.

At some point as he moved forward, he must have recognized the distinctive yellow tips of our firefighter boots and with that he glanced upwards only to see the four of us intently watching him. I recognized him almost immediately because he worked with one of the firefighters from our own department as a house painter on the side. Without so much as cracking a smile, I extended the bottle in my hand and said, "Paul, would you like a cold beverage? You look like you're working hard." For one second, he was speechless, but he recovered quickly. "No, Mac, I'm all set," he said upon recognizing me. Realizing we had let him walk into an embarrassing trap, he didn't waste any time in exiting the premises. It was obvious that he wanted to catch his fellow firefighters before they entered the room and realized what had happened to him. After he left, we laughed for a second, but something similar had surely happened to most of us at one time or another, so it was just our chance to return the favor. Everyone gets a turn at the firehouse—*everyone*.

Brother Dave smiled at the story, then my father came over to see what was so amusing. Somehow, I knew if I revealed that part of the story to him, he wouldn't appreciate it like brother Dave.

Despite being in my mid-thirties, with a family of my own, there was still a part of me that didn't want to feel the disapproval of my father, I couldn't help but wonder if that would ever change. When the phrase "straight as an arrow" was coined, it must have been about someone like Ed McCourt. He was always able to walk the narrow, rocky path he chose without any complaint. If I told him the story that had just been shared with Dave, I knew he would look at his shoes and shake his head, as if to say, you're lucky you didn't get in trouble. But there was another part of the story that I knew he would appreciate, because he always had a great sense of humor.

The incident occurred outside the building after we had finished overhauling the fire. We were in the process of rolling up the hose and undressing the hydrant so we could return to quarters. The feeder line had been removed from the hydrant, but our hydrant connection was still attached and the hydrant was still in the open position. One of the firefighters who had fought the fire and was covered with grime called over to me and said, "Before you shut it down, Doug, let me wash off my hands." It was Joe Nunley, who was working on the ladder company that day, so I stopped what I was doing to give him a chance to rinse off. Once we have our connection on that hydrant, we control the flow of water. There may be two levers or one lever, depending on what hydrant connection you're using. If the lever moves one way, the water flows—just the same as a faucet—and if it's moved the other way, the water stops. Only, unlike a faucet, the opening is much larger and is under much more pressure, quite capable of producing a huge amount of water the instant it is opened. And I do mean a *huge* amount.

Joe positioned himself next to the hydrant—out of the line of fire, you might say—and then gave the lever a tap to crack it open, just a little bit to produce enough water to rinse his hands off. Well, evidently, Joe gave the lever a little too much of a tap and the result was a torrent of water of biblical proportions. What we didn't notice (until we heard a scream) was that a firefighter had been rolling a length of hose about ten feet away and, as luck would have it, he was directly in the crosshairs of the now opened gate. The firefighter let out some unholy ejaculation at the top of his lungs and Joe, realizing his mistake, immediately shut the lever of the gate. The gate had only been opened for a few seconds but the amount of water it produced was incredible. There, standing before us, was our fellow firefighter Bobby Farr with water cascading off every inch of his entire body. For a moment, he just examined his thoroughly drenched condition with a stunned look on his face and his mouth slightly agape. Then he looked back up towards Joe, who was standing by the hydrant with an embarrassed look on his face—although there was also a glimmer of a smile at the sight of Bobby's fate. After regaining his composure, Bob said disgustedly, "I managed to stay fairly dry through this fire, Joe, but now I feel like I went for a swim. I can only hope that I have a complete change of clothes back at the station." It was one of those classic firefighting moments that turns into rich material for one liners around the firehouse for weeks afterwards.

My father and brother shared a laugh at the end of the story, but then my brother added, "I've got one that tops that by a mile. It was the exact same situation as the one you described, only the result was ten times worse." I had triggered that competitive firefighter storytelling mechanism that always seems to occur when firefighters get together, and my brother, Dave, proceeded to tell us his own watery tale.

"We had a house fire in the middle of the night, and after we finished with it I was the one sent to break down the hydrant.

The hydrant was located about four hundred feet down the street. Far away from the house and the flashing lights of the apparatus, as well as, the usual onlookers who show up to watch the show in the middle of the night. I had the same thought as your buddy Joe. Since I was going to shut down the hydrant and take the gate off, I may as well crack open the valve and wash the grime off my hands, maybe wipe my face and get a little cooled off while I had the chance.

"So without giving it another thought, I gave the lever on the valve a little tap to get enough water flowing to rinse off. The same exact thing happened, Doug. The valve opened up almost all the way, the water came out like it was shot out of a cannon. As I jumped back to avoid getting drenched, I was stunned to hear a person scream at the top of their lungs!

"There, standing in the middle of the street, was a man dressed in a business suit no less, with a briefcase in his hand. He just happened to be perfectly in line with the open gate. It wasn't a second before I rushed to close the open gate but it didn't matter because he was soaked from head to foot, with an utter look of disbelief on his face!

"I'm thinking to myself, where the hell did he come from? I mean, it's like four-thirty in the morning and out of nowhere, for the one instant I crack the valve open, which produces this huge blast of water, a man in a three-piece suit magically appears and is directly in the line of fire. It was unbelievable! I couldn't even think of anything to say, so finally I just looked at him and said, 'Geez, pal, I hope I didn't screw you up.'

"He looked back at me shaking his head and in a disgusted tone said, 'Oh no, you didn't screw me up, not at all. I only have to be on a plane leaving for Chicago in an hour, that's all!' Then he turned abruptly and walked off into the night and left me standing there feeling like a complete fool."

I had to admit that did beat my story. My father and I had a good laugh as we could only imagine the poor man's dilemma as well as the embarrassment my brother must have felt. The man probably went to the airport drenched to the bone because he didn't have enough time to return home to change. After we had our laugh, my father looked at the two of us and said, "I've got one that tops that by a mile." Now, I knew if my father made a statement like that, then the story had to be outrageous, because he wasn't one who would make an idle boast. So he had our complete attention as he began his own liquid tale.

"I was working on an engine company with Jimmy Devine and Joe Small, one night. We had finished fighting a house fire and had received the unenviable assignment of serving as the fire watch detail to make sure there was no rekindle. We still had the hydrant hooked up to our pump, but the hydrant was around the corner so we couldn't see it. It was about three-thirty or four o'clock in the morning and we were all pretty tired by this time. The three of us decided that each one would take a turn watching the building, while the other two tried to catch a little shut-eye, because it was going to be a long, boring wait until shift change.

"After sitting there for awhile, someone knocked on the passenger door of the engine, so Joe rolled down the window to see what they wanted. A man was standing there in the blackness of the night and he asked us if we knew that the hydrant around the corner was leaking? Well, that wasn't very big news because all hydrants leak. The hydrant, the valve, the hose, something is always leaking water around the hydrant. So we told the gentleman not to worry about it. We knew it was leaking and there was nothing that could be done about it. It was just a matter of old equipment and poorly maintained hydrants, but we told him that we appreciated his concern. He looked at us slightly surprised and then disappeared back into the night. After he left, the three of us discussed why in the name of God this fellow was wandering around in the wee hours of the morning providing helpful hints to firefighters. Then we grumbled about how it was bad enough that each of us had to take turns watching a darkened house to make sure it didn't rekindle, we certainly didn't need some *Helpful Henry* dropping by to interrupt the forty winks that we might be lucky enough to catch. After a brief discussion about our unexpected visitor, it was back to the original plan of one awake and two in a stupor.

"About ten minutes went by, and then there was another rap on the door. Again Joe rolled down the window and, lo and behold, it was the same citizen. Once more, he told us that the hydrant around the corner was leaking badly, although he wasn't sure what we could do about it, the water really was spraying all over the place. Joe looked at him straight-faced and said, 'We're aware of it, sir, there's nothing we can do about it! We'll tell the chief when we get back to quarters about this defective equipment and see if we can get some replacements. Thanks for coming down to tell us but there's nothing we can do.' The man shrugged his shoulders with a quizzical look on his face and once again walked off into the night.

"The three of us couldn't understand it. Why would someone hang around, in the middle of the night, at the aftermath of a fire scene when instead they could be home in bed, which is where the three of us would much rather have been! While Joe Small and Jimmy Devine discussed the possible reasons of why this fellow kept pestering them, I began to have second thoughts. 'Maybe we should take a walk back there to check out the hydrant, just to see if there's anything unusual going on,' I said out loud.

"'Come on, Eddie, you know they all leak—every one of them! It's nothing but the normal amount of water spraying that you get from any hydrant. It probably looks like a lot to him because he doesn't realize that they all leak like that!' Joe replied, shaking his head in frustration.

"'Just in case, though,' I said to them. 'To at least put my mind at ease.'

"'Okay, Eddie,' Joe said. 'If it will give you peace of mind, let's go back and check it out just to be sure.'

"So the three of us, reluctantly, got out of the truck and walked down the street and around the corner to where the hydrant was located. When we turned the corner and the hydrant finally came into view the only thing I could say was, 'Oh, my God!' There was a stream of water shooting out of the hydrant up through the dark of the night like it was shot from a water cannon!

"The hydrant had been dressed with a Y connection, which has two gates leading from it. One of the gates was tied into the line that was feeding our pump, the other gate was unoccupied but was available if we had needed more water at the fire. Well, some practical joker had completely opened the available gate, and as Murphy's Law would have it, this particular hydrant had tremendous water pressure. We couldn't have got a more powerful stream with one of our own deck guns. To make matters worse, because the gate was tipped slightly upward the stream was arcing high through the air, and on the other side of the street it was pummeling a two-family home.

"Immediately, we shut down the gate and looked across the street at the two family in disbelief. Apparently, nobody was home, so no one had complained about the incredible amount of water drenching the front of the house. Only a good Samaritan, who happened to be awake at three in the morning, had been there to report the situation to the firefighters on the scene—a couple of times!

"The three of us walked across the street hoping that the water hadn't done anything more than give the house a good pressure washing. But to our dismay, when I looked up at the second floor where the water had been deflecting off the house, I could see it had blown out a window and some of the water must have entered into the house.

"Oh no, I thought to myself, I hope not much of it made its way into the house. But when I walked up the front stairs and reached the door to the house, that question was answered immediately. There was a small river of water pouring out from underneath the front door that led to the second floor of the house. Not only had the water entered the second floor, it had done so with such volume that it turned the staircase into a waterfall and the front door into a dam."

Shaking his head slowly as he recalled the scene, he continued, "I could only imagine the amount of damage that had been done to the house. There was probably more damage done by the *leaky hydrant* than at the house down the street that had been on fire. Oh God, I thought, how am I going to explain this! Here we were specifically left at the scene to make sure everything was secure. All I could think of were the foolish answers we gave the good Samaritan. He was only trying to tip us off as to what was going on around the corner at the hydrant. 'Don't worry about it, they all leak.' Boy, did that answer sound absurd, as I stood there staring at the house. We questioned him and his motivations. I could only imagine the story he'd share with his neighbors about us: the three nitwits who told him there was nothing to worry about.

"When the day shift relieved us, I hustled back to the station hoping to exit the premises before the chief showed up for work. Unfortunately, bad news doesn't travel faster anywhere than it does at the fire department. When I was almost out of the station door an announcement was made over the loudspeaker, 'Lt. McCourt, the chief would like to see you before you go home.'"

"What did he say dad?" I asked smiling, I couldn't help myself. "He just wanted to know how something like that could have happened and I told him that I had no idea. Some fool's idea of a joke was all I could come up with."

My father stood there looking down at the ground. I could see him reliving the embarrassment of it, as if he were still standing in the chief's office feeling red in the face. He was wearing the same expression I would have received if I had told him about the fortuitous beverage acquisition we had made the previous night at our house fire. He was right, his story did top ours. At that moment, someone called to us from across the way, "Come on over, guys, they're bringing in the birthday cake." It was time to join everyone else and sing a chorus to our little birthday celebrant. Hopefully, it wouldn't be too long, I thought to myself, before I could go home and take a much needed nap. The combination of strong coffee and firefighting stories had helped me make it through the party without getting a bad case of whiplash from sleep deprivation.

As years go by, I realize how lucky the three of us were to share the same profession. We had something in common and it seemed to bring us closer together. At family gatherings, we would inevitably be drawn into these storytelling contests. My father had indeed won the battle of our hydrant mishaps, but with twenty-five years of service, he had a far deeper well to draw on. In fact, at that point in time of our lives, he had more time on the job than my brother and I combined, but the future certainly would hold more chances for success and failure for the both of us. Perhaps, at some later date, one of us would have a new water drenching story and my father would have to settle for second or possibly third place. Only time would tell, but till then he was hands down the winner of the "Liquid Tales."

CHANGED LIVES

IT'S NOT ALL ABOUT house fires and cats trapped in trees, you learn that real fast. If anyone should have known that, perhaps it should have been me, with a father who was already on the job—although he never was one to talk out of school. So you learn as you go instead. How to handle the downtime around the station, when idleness spawns pettiness and lunacy. How to navigate your way through a house fire and check your emotions at traumatic scenes. How a few words over a loudspeaker can paint awful pictures in your mind: "Respond to a reported suicide," "...to a swimming pool for a possible drowning," "...to a report of a pedestrian hit by a train." The list goes on and on. It's like some morbid picture album trapped in your head filled with gruesome images. These scenes weren't encountered every day, but there were more than enough, and sometimes occurring without even a warning.

When I first joined the fire department, I was assigned to Group 4 at headquarters as an extra man. As the low man on the totem pole, I was used as your basic back-step man, while training to become an EMT. It gave all the senior men a chance to abuse me, since I held the distinction of being the most junior man on the entire department. "Down with the whale dung on the bottom of the ocean," is how my comrades imaginatively described my lowly position. The Engine 1 driver told me he had spent more time driving the pump in reverse than I had spent on the job. I couldn't appreciate it then, but later I found out for myself what absolute delight one can find in baptizing new recruits.

Voluntarily, I matriculated into an EMT course to earn my ticket, as they say, so I could ride the rescue. Perhaps "volunteer" is not the right word, since I had been told that if I didn't receive an EMT status in my first year on the job, which was a probationary period, that my employment may well be terminated. Naturally, this information weighed heavily on my decision to "volunteer" for the EMT course. The rescue truck had the highest burnout rate of any job on the fire department. As each new member became certified to ride the rescue, it seemed a more senior member would breathe a sigh of relief and move on to another job. This would enable them to work on a pump or a ladder, doing more traditional firefighting. My father had spent twelve years on a rescue unit, in another city, so I wasn't going to complain about the requirements of becoming an EMT. I took the course, got my ticket and rode the rescue for three years. At the end of that time, I must tell you, I wondered how my father ever stayed on the rescue for twelve years. There were several firefighters on our department that had been with the rescue company for a dozen years or more as well. They were held in high regard in the department. Over the years, at many catastrophic rescue scenes, my fellow firefighters and I had breathed a collective sigh of relief on seeing one of these veterans emerge from the rescue, knowing the success of the call might depend solely upon them.

This particular aspect of firefighting was not something I had been previously made aware of, even though, as I said, my own father had worked on a rescue company for so many years. It was a topic that he never really talked about at home. Most firefighters are willing to discuss the routine rescue calls, the same as they would fire calls. Conversely, this is not true of the tragedies where the human suffering is so great that lives have been changed forever—not only the victims, but sometimes, the firefighters as well. These calls are seldom discussed, if ever, and then only among individuals with similar experiences. I worked with certain firefighters for years before they revealed to me the details of a particularly brutal call that they had witnessed, and even then it was told in a quiet voice, as if they were revealing to you some dark secret. After suffering through some of the same scenes, it's easy to understand why no one wishes to relive them. It's like when you get deathly sick after eating a certain food and for such a long time afterwards you feel revulsion at the slightest sight or smell of it. Well, gruesome calls are very similar in the way your psyche is affected. After witnessing a disturbing scene, it's a normal human reaction to try to clear the revolting pictures from your mind. Henceforth, you do not choose to discuss it simply because it touches a part of you with that same sickening feeling that you experienced on that day.

I was working on Engine 3 at the time with Lieutenant Philly Petrino and Fenway Frank. It was a three-man pump that covered the east side of town. A call was received to respond to a residential house for some debris burning on the lawn. A typical nuisance call, we all thought, as the pump headed out the door. The only thing notable, at the time, was that we were in the middle of preparing lunch, so we had to shut off all the appliances before we left. Otherwise, we might return to a pile of smoldering ashes and that fire report definitely wouldn't reflect well on the fire prevention aspect of our job. The absence of smoke or fire alarms in the building would make a great headline in the local newspaper. There must be some sort of constitutional provision for double standards in city charters.

On the way to the call, the dispatcher struck a box on the incident, which would now send a full response to the scene. In our city, that would mean two pumps, a ladder truck and a rescue company would be dispatched to the same address. The dispatcher had been receiving calls from concerned citizens who seemed overly excited about a little debris burning on a lawn. As we arrived, I remember seeing a police cruiser parked directly in front of the house and the pile of debris still smoking next to him on the lawn. The officer looked disconcerted, but everything seemed like it was under control. When the officer caught a glimpse of us, he motioned for us to come quickly and his face appeared panic-stricken. There had to be something else happening that I wasn't seeing, I thought to myself. As I looked at the smoking mound again, I realized for the first time it wasn't a pile of debris at all, but instead the body of a very badly burned person. For a second, Phil and I were too stunned to react, at that same moment our rescue company turned the corner and approached the scene. As we flagged them over to where we were standing, it was a relief to see one of the most experienced rescue personnel in the city was on duty that day.

To everybody who arrived, it was a shocking scene. The alleged debris was the body of a young man. His clothes were completely burned off, except for the soles of his work boots which were still smoking heavily. In fact, his whole body was smoking. His hair was gone, his eyebrows were gone, his eyelids had been destroyed leaving him wild eyed and staring at the sky. There was a frail old woman standing on the front porch of the house screaming and shaking uncontrollably. For a moment, all of us were almost dazed as we began to realize the tragedy that now confronted us. The police officer was barely able to convey what had happened. This young man in some sort of emotional breakdown had decided to come home with a five-gallon can of gas and set himself on fire in front of his mother. The police officer, who had been the first on the scene, used a small foam fire extinguisher from his cruiser to try to smother the flames. The officer was pale as a ghost and visibly upset. Yet, in spite of this, he went to the aid of the boy's mother who was coming apart at the seams.

Amazingly, the young man was still alive, and, with his distraught mother watching in horror, we worked frantically to get him ready for transport to the hospital. Although most of us had treated burn victims before, nobody had ever seen anything this extensive. Dick Crowell was the senior EMT on the rescue that day, he was one of those veterans who had a dozen years under his belt. If he felt the pressure of our collective group staring at him, he certainly didn't show it. During traumatic calls like this, he was one cool customer—though afterwards he'd agonize over every detail.

The young man was lying on his back with his arms and knees raised in the fetal position, a reflexive reaction to the trauma. Our most pressing problem was his body temperature, which was so hot it was still smoking. We were confounded as to how to rid his body of the extreme heat that was still lingering. All the sterile water that was carried on the rescue had been exhausted and still his body was almost too hot to touch. Finally, we pulled a booster line off Engine 3 and began sprinkling his body with water from the pump. This definitely wasn't how the textbook said it should be done, only sterile water was supposed to be used, but what we had wasn't enough and we didn't know what else to do. Dick made sure we all donned protective latex gloves before attempting to lift the victim on to the burn sheet. Contamination was big problem with burn victims, since the protective layer of outer skin is gone. I remember how shocking it was to actually touch him. His skin was hard like a frankfurter that had been cooked on a grill. God, I was so afraid that my fingers might do even more damage as we lifted him on the burn sheet. On calls like that you become a robot: rigid with the self-control needed to perform your job. Not looking into his unblinking eyes, not listening to the gurgling sounds coming from his chest, but still it was hard not to be overwhelmed by it all. Sometimes, these situations are dropped on you so quickly it's hard to prepare yourself mentally for the images that seem to attack your mind.

As a former EMT, I stayed with the rescue company for the ride to the hospital. On the bad calls, we always brought an extra man in case CPR needed to be administered while in transit. Fenway and Philly would follow with Engine 3 and meet us at the emergency room. As basic EMTs, there wasn't much we could do but give our patient oxygen and keep his body free from contamination. While en route, I took a long look at the devastation the young man had inflicted on himself. I looked at Dick and asked him, "Can anyone survive burns this severe?" He shook his head and mouthed the words, "I don't think so." Then he put his forefinger to his lips and motioned me not to say anymore, adding softly, "Dougie, I'm not sure if he can hear us or not."

I hadn't thought for a moment that he would be able to hear me, but now the thought that he may have heard me pronounce his death sentence filled me with remorse. I had to say something to him. Something to atone for my thoughtless words, whether he could hear me or not. Staring into his unblinking eyes, I told him we'd do everything we could for him and that in less than a minute he'd be in the hands of the hospital staff and they were all prepared for his arrival. "I'll say a prayer for you," I added. Then quietly I prayed, as I sat looking at the terrible tragedy that was lying before us. It may have well been the only real medicine he received from us that day. Still humbled by the caution that Dick had given me, I made no further reference to our patient's condition.

When we transferred him at the emergency room to a hospital cot, I dreaded touching his charred body again. It was such a selfish thought. But seeing and touching this young man, who was so horribly burned, was hard for the mind to accept. There was a great weight lifted off us, when the staff at the emergency room took charge of our patient and released us to return to our stations. The first thing Phil and I did, on returning to our station, was take the lunch we had been preparing before we left and throw it away. Fenway, on the other hand, took the chili he had been eating, reheated it in the microwave, then proceeded to sit down and finish his meal, as if nothing had happened. I stood between him and the television he was watching, staring at him, until he finally asked, "What's the matter?" I told him that he was one sick individual and I asked him how in the name of God could he eat after the call we had just suffered through? He simply said, "Doug, ever since Vietnam, none of that bothers me anymore." I guess the mind steels itself against the shock of seeing such atrocities. Although, I think you lose a little something in the process.

A few hours later, we received a call from Dick Crowell informing us that the young man had died. Amazingly, he had survived for several hours. The human body is a remarkable thing. That night I found sleep elusive. The pictures and sounds of the day wouldn't leave my mind in peace. Finally, I abandoned the bed and sought out my easy chair and a brown bottle—once more, turning to the poor man's cure for some comfort. Although, by this time, I was beginning to wonder if it was more of a curse than a cure. As I sat there examining the contents of my glass, I recalled an event that occurred some twenty years ago. Barely a teenager at the time, I didn't fully comprehend what had taken place, but today's events enabled me to see what had happened back then in a new light.

It was a weekend afternoon and my mother was setting up the table for lunch. As usual, she required that all of us sit down and eat together. After a short time, someone inquired as to the whereabouts of our dad, since he always sat down to eat with us when he was home. My mother told us, "He had a rough shift at the fire department and he's in the bedroom taking a nap." Later in the day, I saw my father a few times, as he got up to get a drink of water or to use the bathroom, but each time without a word. Then he'd quickly return to the bedroom and close the door behind him. At supper, once again, his seat was empty.

By this time, my mother realized she needed to give us an explanation. She told us that on his last shift, Dad had responded to a call for an explosion in the southern part of the city. Upon arriving, they were confronted with a terrible tragedy. Three young boys had been playing with matches, and as a childish prank they had decided to drop some of them down the fuel tank of an abandoned truck. The results had been horrific. The fumes in the tank had ignited, enveloping the boys in an exploding ball of fire. The situation would require more than one rescue on the scene and everyone would need to work feverishly, if the boys were to be saved from the consequences of their terrible mistake.

Since the fire rescue was on the scene first, they would attend and transport the victim in the most dire condition, while their fellow firefighters treated the remaining victims and readied them for newly arriving ambulances. My father, being a veteran EMT, attended the poor boy on the ride to the hospital. He was just a kid, no more than twelve years old. The blast had literally ripped the clothes from him and the ensuing fire had burned a major portion of his body. He was in severe shock and thankfully felt little pain, even though in places his flesh was completely torn open. Ironically, he was more concerned about the trouble that awaited him at home for playing with matches, rather than the grievous extent of his own injuries. My father tried to console him, saying he would tell his parents it was an accident. He assured the boy he could smooth things over, and asked him not to worry. The boy asked if he could raise his arms, so he could see for himself the condition of his wounds. There was no reason for him to see the horrible sight, instead, my father tried to calm his panic-stricken mind. The mere sight of his injuries would have been devastating to the boy, so he cajoled him by saying the sterile dressing couldn't be disturbed. As a father of four children, that were more or less the same ages as these boys so terribly injured, his heart was breaking. All these emotions had to be hidden behind a poker face or a reassuring smile if necessary, so the boy in front of him wouldn't sense how truly desperate things were at that moment.

Even though you always hope for a miracle, as an EMT with years of experience, he knew in his heart the child probably wouldn't survive more than a few hours. If there was nothing else that could be done, then at least he could make the boy as calm and cared for as possible. Until the moment they departed from the hospital, every member of the rescue company displayed a kindness and humanity that can't be found in any of Webster's definition of the word "firefighter." I'm sure there was a solemn atmosphere until the end of their shift that day. Each man trying to deal with emotions that refuse to be denied.

My mother didn't tell us the whole story at the time. She only told us the basic components, and as a caution about never using matches around something flammable. Gradually, my father began to emerge from the bedroom for brief periods of time, and later the next day, he was in his usual place at the dinner table, although still abnormally quiet. He was very much like his mother, Mary Josephine McCourt, who always seemed able to bear emotional pain without saying a word. A family trait, I guess. I'm not sure if that was a good thing or a bad thing, perhaps a little of both.

As I sat looking into the amber water in my glass, I thought of my father the teetotaler, and how lonely the weary weight of the world must have felt that day. I could feel a sudden wave of emotion sweeping over me. I wasn't sure if it was for my father, myself, or maybe just the horrible nature of the tragedies.

I rode the rescue for three years and I was overjoyed when I finally had enough seniority to win a bid for an engine company. It still amazes me that anyone can spend a dozen years, or more, on a rescue company, but thank God, they do. There is no question that sometimes firefighters get emotionally involved at a call. Is that a bad thing? Maybe for the emotional wellbeing of the firefighter, but the empathy for the victims sharpens your senses and brings out unnatural courage, and the victims benefit from this emotional adrenaline. It might appear to bystanders that sometimes firefighters risk an awful lot for a stranger, but at that moment, we may have needed to take that same risk for ourselves. We can only pray that no one dear to us is ever in desperate need of the service of a rescue company, but if they are, I hope that men like Ed McCourt and Dick Crowell are the ones who answer the call.

1617

I
T WAS ONE OF those rare weeks when the golden days of
summer approached perfection. We stayed in a cottage
overlooking the shimmering waters of Chandler's Bay
in Jonesport. A perfect example of what Maine resembled in
previous times. The quiet fishing village with plenty of space—
authentic "Downeast." It was a week spent in an hypnotic trance,
mesmerized by a fractured ocean full of sequins. But like every
vacation spent in that piece of heaven, it ended much too soon
and the next day I'd be back at the firehouse.

A lot happens in what amounts to just twelve days away
from the fire department. All the misdeeds and crazy calls wait
patiently for fresh ears to hear their stories.

No one's ears were more eager than mine and I smiled in
anticipation of a good dose of nonsense. There was only one
thing bothering me as I arrived at Engine 3, and that was the distinct odor of burning brush streaming through my open window.
Even though I was returning to work, it wasn't actual *work* that I
had hoped to find.

Firefighters employed in the concrete jungles where trees are
an endangered species might think, "Big deal, a brush fire." Well,

it can be a big deal. It can mean endless hours of eating smoke, dragging hose and dehydrating yourself in the summer's heat intensified by the burning brush. If you're lucky enough to be successful, you can enjoy the immense satisfaction of knowing that a few shrubs have been saved from incineration. Not much to bask in as you roll up endless lengths of hose to reload the pump.

When I walked into the day room, Phil smiled and said, "Welcome back, stranger."

Sitting across the room from him reading a newspaper was Kevin Kelly, a firefighter that I hadn't worked a shift with in years. "What's up, K.K.?" I asked, wondering how he ended up at E3.

"Overtime," he answered with a grin. There's something about that word "overtime" that makes a firefighter smile.

"He might earn it, too," Phil said with a grimace.

"Is the brush that bad?" I asked.

"Let's just say you picked a good week to go away, Doug. We've been running ever since you left."

"Well, it's nice to hear I missed some of it," I replied.

As I sat there drinking my first cup of coffee and perusing the front page of the paper, the intercom sounded, "Attention Engine 3, respond to a report of brush in the vicinity of the Ripley school."

I didn't miss enough, I thought to myself as we headed to the piece.

The three of us accepted the news with quiet resignation because the smell of brush was everywhere. To be honest, since I was the chauffeur Phil and Kevin would do most of the dirty work, which I didn't mind at all, but it did require the disposal of a perfectly good cup of coffee.

Upon arrival at the scene, we could see that the entire hill behind the elementary school was burning. In fact, it extended well beyond what we could see through the smoky haze. Phil made a report to the dispatcher, "We're off at the scene, we have extensive brush." Concerned that burning embers might endanger the school, the chief sent the ladder company to assist on the call. The "Truckees" were never fond of this idea. After all, they were ventilation experts and this was something a hose company should be dealing with. In other words, it was beneath them.

A cemetery was adjacent to the school and by using one of its lanes we were able to situate the pump fairly close to the burning brush. The closer, the better, as far as we were concerned—less distance meant less hose dragging. We tied into a hydrant conveniently located just a few lengths away. This was another big plus because it meant we wouldn't need to shuttle the pump back and forth to refill the tank. Since we had a source of water and the extra manpower, Phil decided to use a larger diameter hose and take full advantage of these unusual circumstances. We ran a 2½-inch line up the hill towards the fire and then split it with a Y connection into two 1½-inch lines. These lines were not only capable of putting out the fire, there was also enough force to dig up the leaves and peat that kept the embers of the fire protected. It might take two men to work each line, but they provided more distance and drowned the hot spots.

Soon we were passing water and with the feeder line, as well as the extra men, things were going good. I settled in at monitoring the pump while my comrades fought the brush fire in two-man teams. One quick call over the radio changed all that: the ladder company was ordered to return to quarters. All of a sudden, the strategy of using larger hose had become a problem. Since we had already gone through the work of laying the lines, we decided to work each line with one man instead of two. We had gained ground and we didn't feel like giving it back by shutting down to rearrange everything. It was hot and the work was heavy, but fortunately for us, Capt. Zinck was on duty that day. Some officers would leave you at a brush fire as if you didn't exist, but not Frank Zinck. He would always show up with a cooler full of beverages and some comestibles, which sounds much tastier than just food.

As advertised, the captain arrived with a trunk-load of assorted drinks packed in ice. When it came to looking after his firefighters, there was none better than Frank Zinck. After Frank left, I called the guys over their portable radios to let them know about the refreshments. It wasn't long before I saw Kevin walking down the hill towards the pump. Even from a distance, I could see he looked tired. Sensing an opportunity, I grabbed a blanket out of a side compartment and spread it on the ground. Quickly, I cracked open a beverage, laid down on the blanket and gazed at the gauges on the pump panel while sipping the drink. K.K. walked around the front of the pump and stopped dead in his tracks.

"You're really breaking your ass watching those gauges, aren't you, McCourt?" he said in a tone full of mocking exaggeration.

Without a glimmer of a smile, I replied, "It's awful. There's no one here to talk to and the glare of the sun is bothering my eyes."

Kevin started laughing in disbelief at the inequity of our situations, since he looked as though he had been dragged through the woods by a runaway horse. He was soaked with sweat and wearing a back support that made his drawers droop a little. There were long black streaks on his face where he had wiped the sweat with hands filthy from the soot.

After looking at the exhausted figure standing in front of me, I took pity and ended the charade. I asked him how he was doing. He launched into a diatribe about the situation.

He vented his frustrations with a list of complaints: why was the ladder company taken away; why use a larger line on a stinking brush fire; why did he take the stupid overtime in the first place when the smell of burning brush was everywhere? Caught up in the moment by K.K.'s litany of grievances, I joined in with gusto. "We should castrate whoever confiscated our manpower. We should let the school burn down into a pile of ashes and become heroes to the Melrose youth. We should take this opportunity to defoliate all this useless greenery by just letting it burn." Phil came up behind us in the middle of our anarchist convention and the three of us started laughing.

It really wasn't funny, though, the three of us were all in our forties and on the back nine of the course of life. The job at hand was brutal and there was no end in sight. I told Kevin that after his break, he'd watch the pump and I'd take over his line. Over his half-hearted objections, I insisted. If we were going to put in a long day, it was only fair that we shared the work—although I wasn't sure where this wellspring of generosity originated. A week's vacation had mellowed me no doubt.

Now it was my turn to sweat, as I followed an inch-and-a-half line that snaked across a charred slope. It didn't take long to realize that using the larger hose was a blessing and a curse. On one hand, it provided the ability to put a solid stream of water over a large area. On the other hand, a person could rearrange their luggage trying to move the damn thing. There aren't too many options when trying to move a hose full of water strung endlessly across a slope in the woods. I was constantly trying to free up hose that somehow found ways to become snagged on every obstacle. To advance the line, I'd throw the nozzle over my shoulder and pull until my body was incapable of gaining another inch. Maybe I was putting too much effort into the process or maybe I'm just a stubborn fool, but either way at the end of the day I felt old and beat-up.

When our shift ended, we went back to the station with the knowledge that despite all of our efforts we'd probably be back tomorrow. As rude as that thought seemed at that moment, it actually turned out to be wishful thinking. After spending a sleepless night with an intense headache, I found myself in the ER the next morning instead of the fire department. The pain was severe, non-prescription medication didn't even touch it. Neither did ice packs nor heat wraps. Only by standing in the shower at five in the morning with the water as hot as I could stand it, did I find any relief—and that was only because it masked the pain. After an excruciating long night, I only wanted one thing at the hospital: painkillers. Pain has a way of putting everything else in your life on hold until you deal with it.

After the usual exam and tests, the doctor decided I had strained my neck and shoulder muscles by pulling on the hose like a mule. A prescription accompanied by a few days' rest was the recommended cure. Everyone who performs manual labor knows that while hard work won't kill you, occasionally, it will beat the crap out of you. After a few days, the headaches went away but the pain in my right shoulder remained. In the meantime, I returned to work, but found it necessary to favor the injured shoulder more and more. On calls that required a little muscle, I noticed some of the firefighters silently wondering what happened to the old Doug. What I didn't know was this injury was different from others I had experienced. Up until this point, any physical problem had been a minor setback: I was about to be humbled. After several months of shoulder pain and headaches, I knew the problem wasn't going to go away. The time had come to seek professional help.

It always amazes me how miraculous modern medicine appears from afar, but when you walk through the door with a list of symptoms, there never seems to be an answer. Instead, there are endless examinations and tests that all have vague results, which lead to further testing. There was even a test that required a number of needles to be inserted into my right arm from my shoulder down to my hand. About halfway into the exam, the doctor asked me how I was doing and for some reason I started laughing. The physician looked at me somewhat confused and asked what I was laughing about. All I could tell him was it seemed absurd to ask me how I was doing when he had been sticking pins in me for the last half-hour. The laughing was not warmly received, but in spite of his demeanor, I couldn't stop myself and I never did understand why he got so perturbed by my reaction. Is there an *inappropriate* way to respond to being stuck with needles?

The headaches and shoulder pain were worse than ever. None of the tests had provided any answers to the source of the problem. Then one day when I stopped to grab a cup of coffee, I ran into an old friend who just happened to be an RN. She asked me how I was doing so I told her, "Not too good." After listening to my complaints, she asked if I had been sent for an MRI. When I told her I hadn't she said, "Doug, you have to go for one, it's the only test that will diagnose the problem." I had to ask her the million-dollar question, "Why hasn't the doctor sent me for one then?"

"They're too expensive," she told me. If it hadn't been for this chance meeting, God knows how long this endless loop would have continued. Armed with this information, I arranged a meeting with my physician who immediately scheduled me for an MRI. It's amazing how persuasive a person can be when they're filled with righteous indignation.

The results of the test told the whole story: I had a cervical disc problem at three different levels. No amount of rest would cure the ruptured discs in my neck. I made an appointment to talk to my union president.

J.P. O'Neil, who had been the union president forever, had just retired. He had been a pit bull of a union officer. J.P. was known throughout the state as somebody who could get things done. A street fighter who used charm when necessary. Bobby Forsey was the new president. He had been groomed for the job by J.P. He was new at the game, but he possessed the qualities you look for in a union leader: steadfast convictions, his word was good and he didn't make promises that he couldn't keep.

Every month since I became a firefighter, union dues had been deducted from my pay. It was something I never really thought much about, but now it meant everything.

An adversarial relationship exists between the union and city hall. Sometime long ago, either the city screwed the union or the union screwed the city and ever since they regard each other's every act with suspicion. My injury would be expensive. It would require the service of high-priced neurosurgeons and paying a firefighter for not coming to work. In an ideal world, this might not be a problem, but in the real world I needed the union like a drowning man needs a life jacket.

As a middle-aged man who was in the middle of things, with children in school and mortgage payments, it was unsettling to know your paycheck could be contested, or even cut off, at any moment. Each time that I needed a medical opinion or procedure, I'd make a request to the city for permission. After a week, if there was no response, which there usually wasn't, I'd call Bobby Forsey and within twenty-four hours my request would be granted. When I needed to see the union attorney, Bobby accompanied me every step of the way, he drove me to the subway station and even paid for my token. To say I'm grateful would be an understatement. For someone like myself who dreads asking anyone for help, he made it easy. In fact, all the members of 1617 did.

The city paid for the opinions of two neurosurgeons and I paid for a third, none of them could put me back on the job. If the operation to fuse the discs was performed, I would not be allowed to return to work. The only thing left was physical therapy. Months of it, and after that something called "Work-Venture," which was a program structured to mimic the job of a firefighter in a clinical environment. They even had me rolling and unrolling lengths of hose. It was a good program and after weeks of improvement I thought I had turned a corner. On a visit to the firehouse, I told everyone that I expected to be back at work in a month.

The hardest part had been visiting the fire stations. On each visit, I was confronted with questions to which I had no answers. "How's the neck?" "Are you doing better?" "When are you coming back to work?" After months of being out on a disability, I was embarrassed by my inability to answer their questions. I thought of my buddy Dick Crowell who had retired with a back injury and how many times I had asked him those same questions. Well, now I was on the other end, learning how exasperating those well-intentioned questions could be. I remember seeing J.P. when he was out with a shoulder injury ducking in and out of the station like he didn't want to be seen, now I knew why.

As time went on, the pressure from city hall began to build. My slot couldn't be filled unless I returned to duty or retired and there is always a manpower shortage at the fire department. But worse than that was the fact that some of my fellow firefighters had family members waiting on the list to get the job. No one would ever say anything, but you knew they couldn't help thinking, "Well, if Doug goes out, there's an opening for my son," or whomever. To make matters worse, any correspondence from the city's attorney required answers from the union's attorney, which was costly.

The presence of two firefighters on the retirement board had allowed me breathing room in a bureaucratic process. Gerry O'Neil and J.P. O'Neil had enough influence over the board to block any premature or forced retirement. Once again, it was members of 1617 supporting one of their own. It wasn't in my nature to let things languish like this: I didn't want to go out the back door on a disability, but I didn't want to remain in limbo forever. The plan was to stay on the job until I was fifty-five and retire with twenty-five years like my father did, but as a friend with a much worse injury than my own told me, "Our plans make God smile."

I told Bobby Forsey to let it go to the disability board and let the panel of doctors decide my fate. Either it would be approved or disapproved. Bobby informed me that I had the right to see the doctors separately instead of all together. He said that historically they tend to be friendlier towards city workers when dealt with one-on-one. But that would require more expenses for the union. "No way," I told him. "Let's just see them all at once and whatever happens, happens. Enough is enough."

The day of the review, I was accompanied by the union's attorney. I brought all the medical documents that I had in my possession. Somehow none of it seemed relevant, instead it was my answers to specific questions they were looking for. What really threw me was they wanted everything in chronological order. I had no idea what the dates were for every therapy or exam I'd been given. The panel waited with concerned expressions as

I looked through my papers and ransacked my memory trying to respond. As I sat there under their scrutiny, I understood why Bobby suggested that I should see them individually. There was an aloof air that I couldn't help but resent as a card-carrying proletarian.

In the end, it all came down to the MRI. The attorney told me after the interview that when one of the surgeons examined the film he began shaking his head and when he showed it to a fellow surgeon, they both shook their heads in agreement. A few weeks later, I received a letter in the mail. It read, "Disability Approved." Even though I wasn't in limbo anymore, there was no joy in the news.

The members of Group 4 had an informal retirement party for me at one of the local pubs. They gave me some gifts and said some nice words. Months later, Local 1617 had their formal retirement party and I stood there amongst a half of dozen firefighters who were retiring. It was a good group, some of the finest men I had worked with, but when they read the years of service of each retiree I couldn't help but feel diminished.

As I left the retirement party that night with my mementos, accompanied by handshakes and well wishes, I couldn't help but feel a sense of melancholy that now it was all in the past.

A few years later, I was required to take a physical exam—it's required of all personnel who go out on a disability. I was told to bring all my post-retirement medical history. This time I made a point of knowing the chronological sequence, so I wouldn't be made a fool of again. A state-appointed physician took my records, sat me on the end of an examination table and proceeded to perform a cursory examination. Then he asked me the one question I don't think anyone else in the entire process ever asked me: "How do you feel about your retirement and being unable to return to the fire department?"

The question caught me by surprise and it had an unexpected effect on me. I sat there in silence, wondering how, through all of it, I couldn't recall a single person asking me that. And it was a difficult question to answer. The doctor stood there waiting patiently, but I was speechless. A flood of emotions came over me. My father had died unexpectedly since I had retired and firefighting had been a big part of our lives. My brother was studying for captain and part of his reward would be the right to wear my father's badge number. I even had reoccurring dreams of returning to work, which faded into disappointment as I awoke to reality. The doctor broke the prolonged silence by saying, "Let me take your file, and I'll be back in a few minutes." It was an act of charity.

After he left, I sat there staring at the white walls of the generic room. It was like staring into the waters of Chandler's Bay in Jonesport—only instead of the ocean, it was a fractured sea of memories. When the doctor returned he didn't ask that question again, my reaction had been enough of a response.

In firefighting, there seem to be three stages to your career: the rookie phase, the middle years and retirement. And it seems to happen that fast. In our business, the highest compliment you receive is that you were a "good firefighter." Somehow, the most basic term used to describe our profession ends up being the most important to us. The only resolution to my unfinished work in the fire service is the hope that the men I served with remember me that way.

About the Author

Doug McCourt is retired from the Melrose (MA) Fire Department. He is a Marine Corps vet who also ran a piano-moving business—McCourt Movers—for thirty years. His father, Edward, retired as a captain in the Medford (MA) Fire Department. His brother, David, is a captain and active member of the Medford Fire Department. Doug currently lives in Lynnfield, Massachusetts, with his wife, Joan, and vacations at their summer home in Jonesport, Maine. They have two children, Edward and Leah.

Share your thoughts on the book with the author at
firehousenotes@yahoo.com

Printed in Great Britain
by Amazon